The *Advanced*
PROJECT
MANAGEMENT
OFFICE

A Comprehensive Look
at Function and Implementation

The *Advanced* PROJECT MANAGEMENT OFFICE

A Comprehensive Look at Function and Implementation

Parviz F. Rad
Ginger Levin

S^t_L

ST. LUCIE PRESS

A CRC Press Company
Boca Raton   London   New York   Washington, D.C.

Library of Congress Cataloging-in-Publication Data

Rad, Parviz F., 1942-
  The advanced Project Management Office : a comprehensive look at function and
implementation / by Parviz F. Rad, Ginger Levin.
       p. cm.
  Includes bibliographical references and index.
  ISBN 1-57444-340-2 (alk. paper)
  1. Project management. I. Levin, Ginger. II. Title.

HD69.P75 R33 2002
658.4′04--dc21   2002017127

Visit the CRC Press Web site at www.crcpress.com

© 2002 by CRC Press LLC
St. Lucie Press is an imprint of CRC Press LLC

No claim to original U.S. Government works
International Standard Book Number 1-57444-340-2
Library of Congress Card Number 2002017127
Printed in the United States of America   3 4 5 6 7 8 9 0
Printed on acid-free paper

DEDICATION

To the Memory of My Parents
— Parviz F. Rad

To Morris Levin
— Ginger Levin

PREFACE

The Project Management Office (PMO) is one of the emerging concepts in project management. Most of the current literature focuses on a specific facet of PMO and/or use of the PMO for a specific purpose. There is a need for a comprehensive all-inclusive description of the PMO. The availability of such a full-perspective book will allow project management professionals to select the features most appropriate and relevant to the issues at hand, while keeping the full PMO activities in perspective.

This book identifies the basic elements of a PMO in an easy-to-read format. It covers the motivations for establishing a PMO, such as project performance, project manager competency, or the organizational desire to excel. Short-term functions and long-term functions are identified and discussed.

Chapter 1 provides a general introduction. Chapter 2 presents two separate, but related, models that deal with the evaluation of project performance from the vantage point of the client as well as from the vantage point of the project team. Structures similar to work breakdown structures (WBS) are developed for use in the process of evaluating the project performance during the life cycle of the project. Guidelines for increasingly detailed evaluations are provided. Chapter 3 addresses the reasons for, and examples of, mal-performance of projects. Remedy plans for runaway projects are presented in some detail.

Chapter 4 catalogs the skills of the project manager and the project management team, as well as the PMO team. For visualization purposes, the skills are grouped into two major categories: quantitative and qualitative. Detailed tables present the duties performed by position and the knowledge and competency requirements. Chapter 5 describes organizational project management maturity, providing another basis for the desirability of the PMO, and ultimately, an exceptionally useful tool for evaluating the operational effectiveness of a PMO.

Chapters 6 and 7 detail the major functions of the PMO: promoting, archiving, clearinghousing, training, mentoring, consulting, and augmenting. These functions are grouped and described in two separate categories: project-focused functions and enterprise-oriented functions. Project-focused functions provide quick results and are often used in crisis management situations. In contrast, enterprise-oriented functions are intended for long-term impact. With this backdrop, plans for the effective implementation of a PMO are discussed. The PMO advantages and implementation philosophies are presented and described. Planning guidelines and facilitative worksheets are included and discussed. Chapter 8 describes the PMO's role in the area of professional responsibility.

Parviz F. Rad
Ginger Levin

ABOUT THE AUTHORS

Parviz F. Rad, Ph.D., is a Distinguished Service Professor and Director of Project Management Program at Stevens Institute of Technology. He holds an M.Sc. from The Ohio State University and a Ph.D. from Massachusetts Institute of Technology. He has more than 30 years of professional experience in governmental, industrial, and academic capacities. He has participated in project management activities and in development and enhancement of quantitative tools in project management in a multitude of disciplines including software development, construction, and pharmaceutical research.

Dr. Rad has authored and coauthored more than 50 publications in the areas of engineering and project management. Dr. Rad has been recognized as a Professional Civil Engineer, Certified Cost Engineer, and as a Project Management Professional.

Ginger Levin, D.P.A., is a consultant in project management with more than 25 years of professional experience in the public and private sectors. She earned her B.B.A. from Wake Forest University and her M.S.A. and D.P.A. from The George Washington University, where she also received the outstanding dissertation award.

For the past 6 years, Dr. Levin has been active in project management maturity at the organizational and personal levels and has participated in the development of six maturity models. She has worked in or supported PMOs at First USA, Citibank, UPS, the National Finance Center of the USDA, and the Federal Aviation Administration. Prior to her consulting work, Dr. Levin held positions of increasing responsibility with the federal government.

CONTENTS

1

INTRODUCTION

1.1 BACKGROUND

One of the most significant developments in recent years has been the formalization of the implementation of the Project Management Office (PMO) and its increased importance to the organization. Because of the beneficial effects of implementing a PMO, increasingly more organizations opt to establish a PMO to support and manage the project management efforts. No longer is it solely an organization with staff to provide support for schedule development and monitoring activities and the use of project management software on a single large project; rather, it is now becoming an essential component for the future success of the organization. Such a trend will only continue, as projects become a way of life for more and more organizations, and more organizations move toward implementation of the management by projects philosophy.

The PMO has been described as a group of individuals authorized to speak for a project (Cleland and Kerzner, 1985) and as a means of nurturing project management capabilities from the perspective of improved methods and procedures (Block, 1998; Frame and Block, 1998). In many ways, the PMO is akin to the discipline offices, such as civil engineering, mechanical engineering, computer engineering, etc., that are found in engineering design houses. The analog for the PMO in pharmaceutical research can be found in departments such as cardiovascular, gastrointestinal, and neurosciences. The PMO is referred to by different titles such as Project Office, Project Support Office, Project Management Office, Project Management Group, Project Management Center of Excellence, or Directorate of Project Management. Independent of the operational title, a PMO is the organizational entity with full-time personnel to provide a focal point for the discipline of project management.

1.2 PMO PROMISES

Among other things, the PMO provides an infrastructure for tools and expertise in the area of project management. To serve the ongoing success of organizational projects and to highlight the benefits of formalized project management, the PMO maintains a clearinghouse for project management best practices. To serve the immediate project needs, the PMO provides an infrastructure for current project managers to deal with difficult situations and establishes an assistance program for the project.

A fully developed PMO has the facility to provide services and organizational focus in core and supporting areas of project management. The PMO's mission and objectives are met by training, consulting, and mentoring the project-related personnel; by augmenting the project teams; and by serving as a clearinghouse for project management best practices, thus promoting communication throughout the organization. A subtle and yet important function of the PMO is to heighten the organizational awareness of the importance of integrating project management procedures and project management culture into the organization. No longer is it appropriate for individual project managers to determine specific project management approaches; instead, the PMO will adopt a standard methodology for use on all projects within the organization. By far, the most exciting functions of the PMO are to instill a project management culture and to facilitate the organizational recognition of the project management profession. As noted by Murphy (1997) the PMO's principal charter is to "help manage the future, not just recalculate the past." The activities of the PMO can be divided into two separate categories, project focused and enterprise oriented, as shown in Figure 1.1. The former is divided into augmenting, mentoring, and consulting. The latter is divided into training, archiving, practicing, and promoting.

The objectives of consulting and mentoring functions are to provide case-specific information and knowledge to the project managers so that they can complete their current projects. The training function is usually intended to impart skills and knowledge to the project managers in order that they can perform their duties more effectively in future projects without the assistance of mentors or consultants. And, at the enterprise

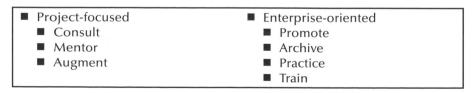

Figure 1.1   Categories of Project Management Office (Functions)

■ Data Clearinghouse	■ Team Building
■ Visibility Center	■ Communications
■ Schedule and Record Meetings	■ Problem Solving
■ Budget and Cost Monitoring	■ Staffing
■ Documentation	■ Process Support
■ Materials and Equipment	■ Project Newsletter

Figure 1.2   Typical PMO Duties

level, the PMO works to ensure project management training is consistent throughout the organization, focusing on the integrity of the curriculum.

There are those circumstances in which the opportunity or time does not allow the implementation of a training program or even the consulting/mentoring process. In these circumstances, a member of the PMO is assigned to a project in order to perform the tasks that seem to be under resourced and/or urgent. As Figure 1.2 shows, typical functions of the PMO include archiving project performance data, compilation of lessons learned, establishment of a knowledge management system, development of checklists, compilation of software reviews, and formulation of documents. As such, the PMO will become a clearinghouse for this information for all project managers. By virtue of providing a centralized point of reference for policies and procedures, the PMO ensures consistency and uniformity to all projects within the organization.

The benefits of a PMO are somewhat subtle but significant. Ideally, the motivation for the establishment of a PMO should come from an organizational desire to excel and an enterprise focus on improvement of the competencies of project managers. Naturally, a PMO is the entity of choice when the organization has the desire to excel in, and set standards for, managing successful projects. A pleasant side effect of this policy would be the enhancement of performance and profitability. However, the impetus for implementation of a PMO is sometimes provided by poor performance of projects. An organization will be a good candidate for a PMO if the implicit and explicit costs of supporting runaway projects are higher than what the organization is willing to absorb. Although different stakeholders may characterize project success factors differently, the need for a PMO is sometimes accentuated by poor performance of key projects, and/or the desire to stabilize runaway projects. The mal-performance of a project, and the need for a PMO, may be reported to the organization by any of its stakeholders, i.e., the client, team members, project manager, supporting organizations, or the accounting department.

The benefits of the PMO include attainment of formalized and consistent project management practices throughout the organization and improvements in project performance. A PMO is a timely and appropriate entity for organizations with multiple projects, multiple contractors, multiple resources, multiple locations, multiple-partner organizations, or complex customer organizations. Further, a PMO can be exceptionally helpful in organizations that have unusual implementation intricacies. The goals of a PMO can vary in urgency and sophistication. If the enterprise has a forward-looking approach to the performance of enterprise projects, the goal would be to set industry standards by way of achieving excellence. Other less ambitious objectives might be to improve divisional project management performance or simply to finish a current project on time and within budget. When implementing a PMO, attention should focus on the portions of the strategic direction of the organization that deal with the project management function.

One would hope that organizational long-range plans include such items as reducing project overruns, improving resource allocation procedures, increasing customer satisfaction, and increasing the delivery speed of projects. The sophistication of the PMO structure and its funding will vary widely depending on whether the overall goals are to improve project-by-project performance, divisional project performance, organizational project performance, or organizational project management maturity, the latter being the most enlightened of these goals. Thus, depending on the circumstances, a PMO might occupy a small corner of the project manager's office and/or a relatively small portion of this manager's time. At the other extreme, it might occupy an entire building with hundreds of employees dedicated to the project mission of the enterprise.

As Figure 1.3 shows, the existence of a PMO allows the organization to conduct formalized and uniform project selection through project portfolio management that is consistent with strategic plans of the organization. Further, the centrality of project planning and project performance information will afford the organization the benefits of a much

- Organizational focal point for
    - Project portfolio management
    - Best practices in project management
    - PM standards and methods
    - Project performance archives
    - Consulting
    - Mentoring
    - Training
    - Quantitative objectives for continuously improving enterprise project management processes

Figure 1.3 PMO Objectives

more effective and efficient coordination of multiple projects in terms of resources, costs, and interfaces. With respect to individual projects, the project manager will be given the luxury of managing the project with an informed view of the past and a logical view of the future. Therefore, runaway projects will be identified and stabilized at the first sign of trouble. Such an informed view might even prevent many of the projects from becoming runaway projects.

The advantages of a PMO include availability of tools, techniques, and principles to facilitate the implementation of quantitative performance measures for project cost, schedule, and scope. To be sensitive to the needs and desires of the client, attention is paid to the final values of the triple constraint, in the light of justifiable and nonjustifiable variances in these constraints. Sometimes, with the misplaced hope of achieving expediency, the treatment of the people issues are forgotten or set aside during the intense implementation activities. Therefore, the tools and techniques developed and maintained by the PMO will also provide schemas to deal with the seemingly nondescript areas of client satisfaction, team attitude, and team behavior.

It is entirely possible that the capabilities described here as those of the PMO currently do exist in the organization either separately or in aggregate; they are just not called a PMO. Organizations that are sensitive to the successful performance of projects may not have to spend any appreciable additional amount of money in establishing a PMO. These organizations are typically in areas such as construction, aerospace, and defense, which have long used standardized approaches and project management software on large projects. On the other hand, the cost of establishing a comprehensive PMO can be a major investment if the organization has never consciously attended to the needs of projects.

1.3 PMO CHARACTERISTICS

The subject matter for the PMO functions includes the entire spectrum of project management competencies. These competencies can be divided into two major categories: those dealing with people and those dealing with things. People-related activities include leadership, conflict management, contract development, negotiations, and communications within the team and outside the team. Things-related activities include skills and tools required in planning and managing scope, estimating costs and schedule, and identifying, analyzing, and managing risks. Tools also include monitoring procedures, auditing checklists, performance metrics, documentation templates, change management, and reporting standards.

Enterprise objectives cover the same knowledge areas as the project objectives, but their beneficial effects will be long term and applicable across the entire organization. These long-term and universal objectives are served through training; collection and dissemination of best practices; development of forms; establishment of policies and standards; and efforts in promoting the professionalism of project management discipline. As for the long-term proactive administrative function, a PMO will develop a knowledge management system for the organization, and maintain an archive for current and previous problems encountered by project managers. A PMO will also maintain a qualified seller list of potential contractors and vendors. Such a list will contain a detailed performance history for each vendor/contractor to be used as a reference in solicitation planning and in contract awards. Additionally, the PMO can provide an inventory of software tools for project management and its allied areas and an inventory of administrative tools, such as checklists and forms for managing and documenting projects.

Project-specific functions of the PMO include facilitation of team-building activities, organizing problem-solving efforts, providing staff augmentation, drafting standards, providing a clearinghouse for project data, dispensing information on project materials and equipment, documenting project activities and project success factors, assisting with budgeting and cost accounting, providing visibility tools such as Web pages and newsletters, organizing project update meetings, and maintaining a central project meeting place, such as a "war room." The PMO will provide guidance, support, and assistance to the project team in managing the quantitative and qualitative issues of the project. The project-focused functions are short-term and remedial functions, and they include providing experts to those who need or desire such services, assisting current project managers, and training future project managers. The functions of the PMO benefit both the project and enterprise project management objectives. These objectives cover immediate assistance to remedy the mal-performance of ongoing projects in the areas of managing scope, cost, quality, schedule, risk, contract, integration, environmental change, communications, and in managing relationships within the team, with the client, and with vendors.

This book presents a comprehensive look at all of the project-focused and enterprise-oriented functions of the PMO. As part of presenting these functions, this book describes quantification of project success, quantification of organizational project management maturity, and assessment of the competency of project personnel.

CONCLUSIONS

The PMO is the organizational entity with the facility to provide services and organizational focus in core and supporting areas of project management. The motivation for the establishment of a PMO might be provided by the organization's desire to excel; however, sometimes the motivation is provided by the failure or near-failure of projects and the associated financial losses to the organization.

2

PROJECT PERFORMANCE FACETS

2.1 OVERVIEW

More and more people are working on projects, and are using project management processes and tools. Everyone wants to improve project success, but many struggle to achieve the desired results. Formal literature and anecdotal data provide many examples of cases where a project falls short of expectations in one or more of the triple constraint items, or in terms of client satisfaction, and yet the project team collectively and officially pronounces the project a success. On other occasions, the team may consider the project a success, while the client pronounces it a failure. The disparity of judgment as to the success or failure of a project might even extend to the team and the client personnel, i.e., the pronouncement of success or failure may not be unanimous among the client personnel or among the project team. Some of the people in this collective group may feel the project was a success, while others may consider failure a better descriptor for the project.

At first glance, this disparity is inexplicable, and it begs the question: How can we work toward project success? One must remember that when someone pronounces a project a success or a failure, the judgment is based on some factual evidence, although not everyone uses the same data. Even when the same data are used all parties do not use the same set of evaluation indices in arriving at a basis of evaluation for the degree of success of a project. Perception of failure and success is sometimes based on unspoken and personal indices, which is why two different people, usually with very different experiences and values, may assess the success of the same project differently. There is a need for a set of performance indices that formalize the project evaluation process and

9

make explicit what is implicit in these seemingly subjective evaluations (Bullen and Rockart, 1981; Dobbins and Donnelly, 1998). There is a need for tools that allow team members and client personnel to formalize the way they evaluate projects. Determining project performance is clearly among the critical roles of the PMO, as one needs to understand exactly what is required and what must be done to achieve excellence in project performance. This chapter provides basic techniques to conduct a uniform and consistent evaluation of projects.

To put the subject in sharper focus, a distinction will be made between the success of the project and the success of the program that sponsored the project. To that end, the vision and the need that necessitated the mobilization of the project will be kept separate from the conduct of the project itself. Therefore, the clarity with which the vision was formed, the precision with which the vision was articulated, and the frequency by which a clearer vision forced the reorientation of the project all will be kept separate from the efficiency by which the original vision, any intermediate visions, and the final vision were achieved by the project. Consequently, if a faulty vision rendered the deliverable of a project unusable, that does not necessarily signify a failure for the project; perhaps it was a failure for the overall program, but not because of the project and not for the project alone. As an example, in a new product development chain, a plant was envisioned and built, but it later was discovered that a competitor had reached the market before this company, and therefore the plant was no longer needed. Clearly, the new product development cycle was a failure, but the efforts of the project team were not necessarily a failure because its members delivered the plant according to specifications, on time, and within budget. Therefore, for the purposes of this book, the success of a project will signify the proper delivery of the envisioned product and not mercenarily the success of the division or product that sponsored the project.

A major unspoken component of quantifying overall project success is the degree of efficacy of a project manager's policies in the area of managing people issues of the project. Sometimes a project can miss some or all of the triple constraints and still be pronounced a success because of the team's positive performance in attending to people issues. Conversely, there might be times that the project is on target with respect to the original scope, cost, and schedule, and yet the client pronounces it a failure because of shortcomings of the team in dealing with people issues. The reason for these seemingly odd pronouncements is that people-related issues will subtly modify the interpretation of quantitative indices of project performance. These people issues include items such as trust, team spirit, morale, responsiveness, punctuality, customer focus, communications, teamwork, conflict resolution, integrity, honesty, professional responsibility, sociability, and flexibility.

Examples of failed, controversial, or marginal projects are difficult to find. Private organizations do not publicize such projects. By and large, the private sector projects that are publicized are those that are successful, at least in the opinion of the upper management of the company. On the other hand, regardless of whether or not the project is considered a success, the project examples that can easily be found are public projects that are funded by Federal and local governments. Examples of such projects are Boston Southeast Expressway, the Springfield Interchange in Virginia, the Pennsylvania Turnpike, Denver Airport, Sydney Opera House, Reagan Office Building, and Woodrow Wilson Bridge in the metropolitan Washington, D.C. area. Accordingly, there is an ongoing debate as to whether, or to what extent, any of these projects was successful.

Using the same set of performance indicators during the entire project life cycle will provide a baseline for informed monitoring of the progress of the project in achieving all of its objectives. This consistent and methodical collection of data will be invaluable in tracking the effectiveness of various project implementation processes during the project phases. Further, the resulting historical data will provide a foundation for continuous improvement in planning future projects. Effective measurement processes can help organizations succeed by enabling them to understand their capabilities and develop plans that can be met by the project team to produce and deliver products and services. Through metrics, people can detect trends and anticipate problems, thus providing better control of costs, reduction of risks, improvements in quality, and greater assurance that business objectives can be met.

It is important to stress that this chapter does not advocate a specific set of attributes and a specific set of rating values, but rather a methodology by which the attributes and their ratings are formalized and documented. The objective of this chapter is not to standardize those indices nor establish their relative weights, but to formalize and highlight a uniform and logical evaluation process. Such a process is a critical role for the PMO. The primary advantage of such formalization is the consistency in evaluation procedures. The secondary advantage is the potential of project-to-project transferability of the resulting values, while maintaining one's own view of success. The structures identified and described here should be modified in concert with organizational culture and priorities and in light of both short- and long-term project management goals of the organization. Finally, the assignment of weights and priorities to the various elements of the structure can be based either on the amount of time and effort that would be necessary to fully manage and deliver a specific element or on the importance of that element.

2.2 TWO DIFFERENT SETS OF ATTRIBUTES

Client and the project team viewpoints on the success of the project are fundamentally different; the former is focused on the deliverables, and the latter is focused on the means by which the deliverables are created. This chapter presents evaluation principles and foundations that highlight and recognize this difference, while providing tools for the client and the team to formalize and document how they measure the elements of success of the project. Use of these structures, or ones similar to them, will facilitate the communication and cooperation between the client and project team throughout the life of the project by quantifying the success attributes from the vantage points of the client and the project team.

The client's success indicators are designed to determine whether or not the final product that was delivered to the client contained a particular feature, whereas the team's success factors tend to focus on whether or not processes, procedures, and tools were in place to facilitate the activities that would ultimately result in the final product. This chapter describes the development of two separate structures, very similar to a work breakdown structure (WBS), to characterize the elements describing the client and the team viewpoints.

The points of reference of the client are the features of the product, although sometimes this perspective may be tempered by behavioral and relationships issues of the project team. There is no question that the team is concerned primarily with the deliverable. But sometimes, as the team plans and executes the project, the activities and processes of the project sidetrack the team to the determent of the deliverables. A similar misplaced importance can occur if the team becomes so focused on the processes, and the deliverables that these processes produce, that the team as a whole might overlook the people issues involved in interrelationships within the team, among the team members, and with the relationship with the client. It is ironic that these relationships in turn will affect the quality and magnitude of the deliverables, albeit in subtle and nondescript ways.

Organizations that traditionally award cost-plus contracts, where the client becomes overly involved in planning the project and in designing all of the activities that are necessary to deliver the final product, run the risk of becoming so consumed with processes that the real mission is almost forgotten. A similar set of circumstances is created in organizations in which the clients conduct extensive micromanagement on projects, where the team members become overly consumed in the prescribed process, and thus place the product at a secondary priority position. The disadvantage of this transfer of focus is that the contractor, or the project team, tends to become focused on following the process prescribed by the client, rather than delivering the final product.

Given that the client and the team generally view project success differently, a set of formalized, explicit, and quantifiable indices will allow the project team and client personnel insight into how the other group views projects. Such indices will allow the team members to develop a needed sensitivity to the client's preferences and priorities. This new outlook is invaluable during the planning, scope development, implementation, and change management of the current project, as it would be in planning of future projects. The relative importance of team factors may change during the life of the project, although the client indicators will be far more stable. For example, the importance of risk management, which is one of the team success factors, will diminish as the project draws to a close. However, the client's primary focus is on the triple constraints, with a secondary focus on people issues, and this focus will stay unchanged throughout the life of the project.

2.3 CLIENT VIEW

The client's focus is on the goals and objectives of the project, and specifically on the scope and quality aspects of the deliverables of the project. Frequently, the cost and schedule attributes of the project are of secondary importance. To some extent, the client does not, and need not, become concerned with all those activities and procedures that are instituted in the process of fabricating, assembling, crafting, or creating the deliverables of the project. The commonly accepted definition of project success attributes, as viewed by the client, refers to the limited product characteristics and areas of product performance that will facilitate successful competitive positioning of the organization; accordingly, success in this limited number of areas will signify success for the project (Bullen and Rockart, 1981; Pinto and Slevin, 1987, 1988; Pinto and Prescott, 1988; Rad and Raghavan, 2000).

From the client's vantage point, the project objectives include attributes and characteristics of the deliverable, such as physical size, capacity, length, height, or strength. The objectives might also involve the achievement of an identifiable level of performance, a prescribed level of quantified reliability, the attainment of a critical speed, the establishment of a quantified level of system availability, the ability to handle a given number of transactions within a defined period of time, or the ability to provide a certain level of quantified customer satisfaction. Other deliverables and objectives might include physical tolerance, physical speed, software tolerance limit, software processing speed, and

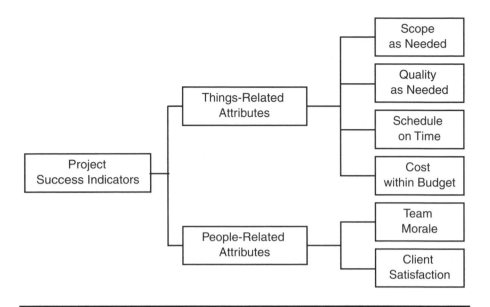

Figure 2.1 Project Success Indicators: Client View

software processing accuracy. Additional deliverable attributes include indicators of surface texture, quantified robustness features, software error frequency, quantified measure of user friendliness of the software, and quantified personnel skills (Figure 2.1).

When the client commissions a project, either for the use of the client or for the use of a stakeholder, the objectives of the project and the characteristics of the deliverables are the basis for measuring the degree of the success of the project. This view of the objectives and deliverables would be held regardless of whether the project will be implemented by an outside organization through a contract or by an internal organization through a mandate or interdepartmental agreements.

The scope and quality of the project have been identified in the literature as the most influential factor among the three components of the triple constraint (Bullen and Rockart, 1981; Pinto and Slevin, 1987, 1988; Pinto and Prescott, 1988; Rad and Raghavan, 2000).

Thus, the success of scope and quality issues tends to overshadow project performance in other areas. Client satisfaction with scope may come from the team's performance in developing a very detailed scope definition during the early stages of the project, or the team's success in implementing a methodical procedure by which the scope was modified, enhanced, and finalized.

With respect to the performance in cost or schedule, the client's perception of success is similar to that of scope and is normally based on the original values, the final values, and the relative magnitude of the variance. Given that some of the variance in cost and schedule is justified, it is only the unjustified portion of the variance that becomes a source of the judgment as to whether or not the project was a success and to what extent. Justified variances will contribute to a perception of success, whereas unjustified variances will signal failure. Sometimes there may be a debate between the team and the client as to whether or not a particular variance is justified. Such differences of perception lead to different determinations of success for the same project. Notwithstanding any shortcomings, the client may consider the scope/quality of the project a success if the client ultimately receives a product that is a close match with the requirements. In many cases, if the client receives a product reasonably close to the original specifications, the costs and schedule overruns will be forgiven or even forgotten as time passes.

From the client's viewpoint, project success can be characterized by project performance in any and all of the elements of the triple constraint. Sometimes, perception of project performance is additionally influenced by indicators that describe overall satisfaction of the client, and by indicators that describe morale of the extended project team including vendors, supporting organizations, and cooperating organizations (Figure 2.1)

Independent of the triple constraint values, the perception of success of a project can be influenced by factors such as the attitude of the project manager, responsiveness of the project team to the client's intermediate requests for minor changes, punctuality in meetings and reports, and that elusive characteristic known as customer focus. Sometimes the project can be pronounced a partial or even a complete success, when the triple constraints indicate very poor performance, but the client satisfaction items are high. In addition, dealing with the set of issues that concern people, some enlightened clients place significant importance on the emotional and morale characteristics of the team members in determining the degree of project success. It is widely accepted that if the project team for one project is demoralized at the delivery of a project, the team's performance in the next project will suffer, almost in compensation for the previous project. More importantly, and given that people issues are much harder to measure and quantify, there may be more protracted debates on whether the team morale is high, and exactly what might have caused the current level of team morale

Thus, the success of the project is primarily measured by the degree to which the desired scope and quality were achieved and by the satisfactory values of project duration and project cost. These items lend themselves to quantification, and hence their performance indices lend themselves to mathematical precision. Naturally, the quantification and accuracy would be meaningful if the project objectives were specified with clarity at the inception, and if the changes to the project environment were tracked and managed methodically throughout the life of the project. The parameters that would influence the pronouncement of success for these attributes are the accuracy of the original value, the acceptability of the final value, and the extent to which the variance is justified by the changes in project constraints and in the constraints of the organizational environment.

Within the context and the tone of this chapter, the client success attributes deal with physical attributes, or with things, and as such can be independent of people issues, even though people issues influence the texture and manner of the delivery of these project features. However, in some cases the client, consciously or subconsciously, places some importance on two categories of the people issues of the project: those dealing with client satisfaction and those dealing with team morale. The items that would influence the client's perception of the success of the project include the team's responsiveness, punctuality, demeanor, trust, adversarial, and communication characteristics. To a lesser extent and much less frequently, enlightened clients consider the team morale during and after the project delivery as an element of project success, particularly if the project is an internal project.

Using a WBS-like structure for the characterization and calculation of success indicators, as viewed by the client, the first level of this structure will have the following elements: things issues and people issues, as shown in Figure 2.1. Things issues include scope, quality, cost, and schedule; these items will be judged on the basis of accuracy, realism, sophistication of the original value, attractiveness, and acceptability of the final value. People issues include client satisfaction and team morale. The relative weight placed on each of these elements will be dependent on organizational objectives, strategic goals, and corporate environments. Figure 2.2 provides a first approximation of these values. Independent of how these attributes are created and ranked, the best results can be achieved if the project is ranked using a consistent and formalized process as frequently as possible throughout the life of the project. Thus, variations in evaluation numbers, which can stem from personal preferences and different viewpoints, will be placed in proper perspective.

In the structures presented in this chapter, the number of points assigned to each element indicates the relative importance of the elements. The total possible number of points that are assigned to the project will then be 500. The reason for this particular distribution is to arrive at a scale of 1 to 5 for the success of the project, somewhat akin to the project maturity ratings assigned to organizations; a brief description of the levels of maturity is provided in Chapter 5. There might be a statistical inference relationship between these two values, although not necessarily a linear deterministic relationship. It is likely that if the majority of projects in an organization

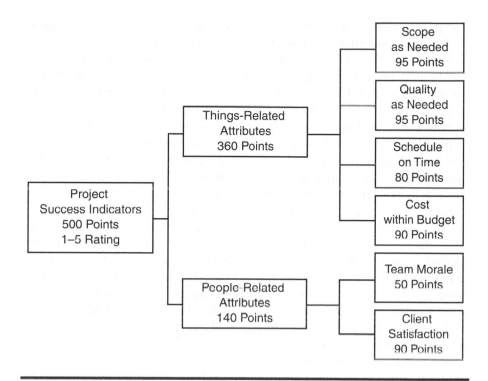

Figure 2.2   Project Success Indicators: Client View, Example, Including Weighting Criteria

are ranked at 3, that particular organization is at level-three maturity. Although this assessment is by inference only, it could nonetheless serve as a good first approximation for the organization maturity. On the other hand, if the organization has achieved a level-three maturity, in all likelihood, most, although not all, of the projects will achieve a rating of 3 or more.

The people issues include team factors, such as team-building activities, conflict management, team spirit, and leadership; client and vendor factors, such as the perception of responsiveness, perception of punctuality, and perception of a positive general demeanor by the contractor; and the efficiency and efficacy of procedures to plan and manage communication among team members and communication with the client and the vendors. It is an important point that factors relating to people issues are difficult to quantify and the resulting quantity is almost always subjective and usually open to debate.

2.4 TEAM VIEW

The primary focus of the project team is the final deliverable of the project. But, the team focuses on the deliverable within the context of the activities and processes that facilitate and ensure the delivery of the desired product in the most cost-effective and efficient manner. The commonly accepted definition of project success attributes, as viewed by the team, refers to the limited project management activity categories that should receive constant and careful attention from the project management team; accordingly, in order for the project to be considered successful, all of the activities indicated by the team factors must be managed well regardless of the phase and regardless of the incremental changes to scope, schedule, and cost (Bullen and Rockart, 1981; Pinto and Slevin, 1987, 1988; Pinto and Prescott, 1988; Rad and Raghavan, 2000). Further, the time spent on these activities, and the impact of these activities on the deliverables, are expected to change during the project life cycle.

Many of the skillful project managers intuitively and informally determine their own success factors. However, if these factors are not explicitly identified and recorded, they will not become part of the formal project management reporting process nor do they become part of the historical project data. Since all project managers are not equal in their skill in identification of success factors, a formalized structure for identification and implementation of success factors will capitalize on the skills of these more experienced and innovative managers for the good of the organization. Therefore, if these intuitive indices become formalized, managerial intuition can become the logical basis, and the structural foundation, for an explicit and standardized evaluation system to be used by all projects and all managers in the organization.

If the success factors are selected on a project-by-project basis, it is entirely possible that they would be a reflection of the project manager's preferences and closely tied to the specific constraints of the project and, as such, evaluation data from this project cannot be easily compared with data from other projects. The manager-specific, or project-specific, success factors might lose their value in terms of applicability to other projects, or even to the same project if the project manager or the team members are changed midstream. To achieve a somewhat universal applicability, a generalized project success evaluation model is needed. The objective in the selection of the structures and categories described here is to achieve comprehensiveness of coverage and applicability to any project, and potentially, in any industry. The advantage of this approach is the availability of benchmarking data across multiple projects, in multiple divisions, in different organizations, and even in various industries.

The defining characteristic of the client indicators is that they deal with the nature and attributes of the delivered product as observed by the client, and not necessarily the actions or non-actions that created the product. By comparison, project managers and members of the extended project team tend to characterize project success in a fundamentally different way. The major difference between client success indicators and team success factors is that client indicators, by and large, focus on the outward appearance of the product, or the performance characteristics of the product, whereas the team's success factors focus on activities and measures that produce the project deliverable. The mission of the project team is to plan the delivery of the desired product through adoption of best practices and consistent procedures, implement those plans in a dynamic environment, and manage all of those issues that influence the performance of the team in delivering the desired product.

Management efforts are considered effective if the desired value for that facet of project management is maintained at the satisfactory level throughout the life of the project. Quantifying success in each one of these items would involve quantifying the effectiveness of achieving the objectives of that particular item. Naturally, the target desired value is not necessarily the original value, but rather the one modified by justified variances. However, in order to assess the success and effectiveness of the manager in achieving the desired objectives, one would need to identify three separate elements in the management of that issue: existence of standardized processes and procedures, consistent conformance of the project team with those procedures, and the efficacy of these procedures. The rationale for this three-part rating system is to determine whether the success of the project manager was by accident or by design. For example, if there are no existing procedures and yet the desired value of that facet is achieved, as much as the occasion is to be celebrated, that performance cannot be expected to be repeated in future projects by this project manager. On the other hand, if the achievement of success for an element is concurrent with these formalized procedures, the likelihood of success for future projects is far greater. Thus, the mission of the project manager and the supporting team is to define and plan each of these components as clearly and carefully as possible, install the plan, monitor the performance of this plan, optimize the plan, and install the optimized plan.

Project success factors, as viewed by the extended project team, can be divided into two major categories: those that deal with things and those that deal with people. The things success factors include quantification of performance of planning procedures, cost management, schedule management, scope management, risk management policies, change management, and integration efforts. The major feature of things issues is that they are somewhat easy to quantify, and therefore, they lend themselves to tabulation, plotting, and evaluation by a variety of metrics.

It is a pivotal point that people issues are intertwined with things issues. It has been observed that a degeneration of any of the items related to people issues will impact the things issues in indirect but profound ways. Nevertheless, basic evaluation factors can be developed for people issues similar to the ones described earlier for things factors. Therefore, the mission of the project manager is to develop processes and procedures for effecting acceptable levels of customer satisfaction, vendor satisfaction, and team morale. Although communication is an essential portion of these activities, attention to people's feelings, priorities, and perceptions are also important in this process.

To quantify the overall success of the project based on project team's elemental success factors, one would first assign a relative importance to things factors and people factors. The relative weight of these two sets of factors depends on organizational culture and on the project manager's background. Regardless, it is a good first approximation that people issues carry a significant weight in the success of the project.

The first level of the evaluation structure for the team-related success factors, as shown in Figure 2.3, includes items related to things and items related to people. The second-level things items are scope, cost, quality, schedule, contract, risk, integration, and reporting. The first four of these elements are clearly things oriented; the second four are primarily things

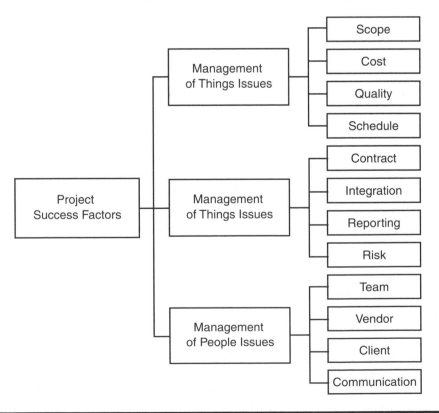

Figure 2.3　Project Success Factors: Team View

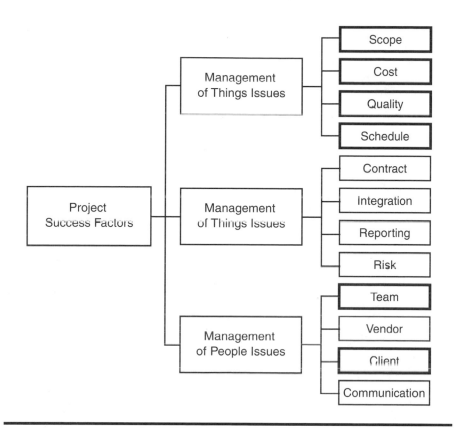

Figure 2.4   Project Success Attributes: Overlap between Team View and Client View

oriented but are partially influenced by people interactions, relationships, communications, etc. Management of procurement, risk, integration, and reporting primarily involves documents, charts, and technical facts but also requires dealing with people from multiple organizations somewhat extensively, more so than cost, schedule, and scope. Therefore, managing these items has a small people issues component attached to it. Additionally, these items tend to be more global and all encompassing, and their field of influence includes scope, cost, schedule, and quality. Therefore, for visualization purposes, the things elements are shown in two separate groups. These values are augmented by elements dealing with project implementation procedures. It is an important point that client attributes are explicitly among the team's important values, even though they are rated differently (Figure 2.4).

All things elements are distinguished by the fact that their quantified status can very easily and conveniently be determined by charts, tables, and graphs. On the other hand, measurement, quantification, and display

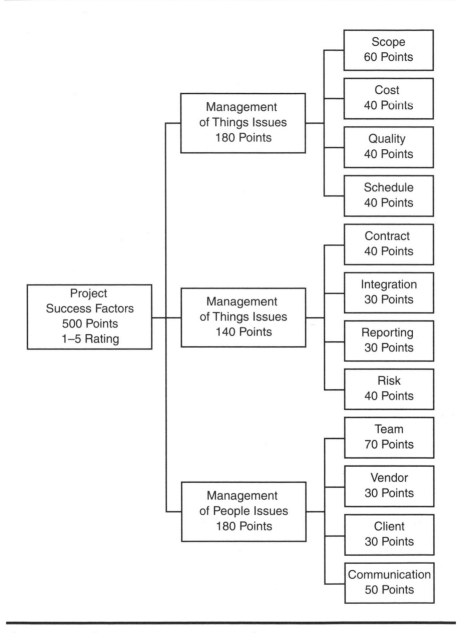

Figure 2.5   Project Success Factors: Team View

of success in people issues are much more subtle, elusive, and subjective. The relative weight placed on each of these elements will depend on organizational objectives, strategic goals, and corporate environments. However, weighting values included in Figure 2.5 can provide a first approximation of these values.

Level-two people elements include managing the team issues, client issues, vendor issues, and communication efforts. The relative weight placed on each of these elements will depend on organizational objectives, strategic goals, and corporate environments. However, weighting values included here can provide a first approximation of these values. Independent of how the weighting values and the corresponding structure are created and ranked, consistency and uniformity will be significantly enhanced if the evaluators have a formalized schema of recognizing the importance of these issues and a methodical approach to measuring the success of managing the people involved with the project. The overall rating of the project success would be derived from rating each of these indicators and then determining the sum total of the individual ratings. Further, using this model, and summarizing the success rating of a large number of the organization's projects, one can obtain a measure of the overall success of the organization in managing projects. Again, this rating would be somewhat akin to an organizational project management maturity rating.

Finally, the number of projects that perform below an acceptable threshold will provide quantified justification for the need for an organizational PMO. This threshold might vary from organization to organization, and it is primarily based on the tolerance of that specific organization to current and future overruns and losses.

Once the success factors that are appropriate for the organization are identified and validated, the foundation for an informed project monitoring process can be established. The availability of these quantified factors will allow the project manager to work with an established archive of historical data in order to keep all aspects of the project within the standards of acceptability of the organization. Such standards and procedures will ultimately improve the probability of the team's success in achieving project goals (Ibbs and Kwak, 1997; Kwak and Dai, 2000).

As in the case of client issues, the points assigned to the team issues will add to 500 points, somewhat in line with a rating of 1 to 5, as is customary for most staged maturity assessments. As with the client success indicators, if the organization is assessed to be at level-four maturity, the average rating of its projects would probably be near or above a 4. However, if several projects are rated at near 4, it does not necessarily mean that the organization has achieved a level-four maturity.

2.5 PROJECT EVALUATION

The project evaluation structures developed in this chapter lend themselves to use in projects on a regular basis or at specified milestones in order to assess an objective view of the performance of the project. Although the detailed definition of the elements of these models can be found in the literature (Anonymous, 1999; Project Management Institute, 1999), a brief listing of their utility is provided here to establish the context. Again, the rating for each of these elements would consider the existence of formalized and consistent practices, full compliance with those practices, and the efficacy of these procedures in achieving the quantified level desired by the client; somewhat independent of whether these desired levels were communicated implicitly or explicitly.

Scope: This term includes procedures for planning the scope, defining the scope, verifying scope, and for an orderly identification and implementation of changes to the scope; procedures for development and enhancement of the WBS.

Quality: This term has two different meanings for project managers: to denote the physical quality of the deliverables as prescribed in the client's specifications or to denote what is known as "good management." The latter refers to best practices in managing the team, managing the documentation, and managing client relations. The second definition overlaps with this model's elements identified as integration, team, vendor, client, and reporting. For the purposes of this model, the quality element refers to the physical attributes of the deliverable product. Accordingly, integration, communication, teamwork, and client relations implicitly deal with good management procedures.

Cost: This term includes all procedures used in developing the original estimate and in enhancing the estimate as more information becomes available; procedures for requesting additional funds if the subsequent estimate exceeds a reasonable threshold; and procedures for requesting additional funds if there are changes in the project environment.

Schedule: This term refers to procedures used in developing the original schedule, hopefully based on the same WBS that was used in the formulation of the cost baseline, and procedures used in updating the schedule in response to resource limitations and the project environment.

Procurement: This term includes procedures used in drafting the contracts used to buy materials and services for the project; procedures involved in administering the contracts and in modifying them in terms of cost, delivery, and duration; and assessment of the efficacy of these procedures.

Risk: This term includes all procedures used in preparing a project risk management plan; identifying the project risks at the onset of the project; analyzing risks, both qualitatively and quantitatively;

and planning responses to key risks; procedures used in monitoring and updating the risk plan; and assessing the efficacy of these plans.

Integration: Project managers use this term to mean three different things: the tasks involved in putting together the physical pieces of the project in order to make a unified deliverable, the tasks involved in facilitating cooperation from other organizational units, and the extent to which cost, schedule, and scope use the same WBS. For the purposes of the model described here, only the second meaning will be applied. Others are addressed implicitly as part of cost, scope, vendor, client, and communication.

Performance Reporting: This term includes all procedures involved in collecting progress data from all project participants, refining them, and reporting them. This element directly assists the effectiveness of the previous items by way of providing timely and accurate information. The rating for this item refers to the availability of forms, logs, databases, and procedures for data collection and reporting, and also includes assessing the efficacy of these procedures (Rad, 2002).

Team: This term encompasses all policies and procedures involved in acquiring the project personnel internally and externally; policies in personnel management including evaluation, reward, recognition, and promotion; and procedures for team formation and for effective team-building tasks. The effectiveness of these policies and procedures is measured by productivity indices, as well as behavioral characteristics such as tardiness, absenteeism, and general morale.

Client: This term refers to all procedures involved in maintaining good relations with the client; those practices that create a general feeling of goodwill and trust among client personnel.

Vendor: This term includes all procedures involved in maintaining goodwill and trust among vendor personnel.

Communication: This term includes procedures for sharing the right amount of information among the right number of people in the project, at the right time, and ensuring that all stakeholders are informed of all pertinent actions.

Using variations of these models, students of one of the authors at the University of Idaho and at The George Washington University examined the performance of several high-profile cases. Summaries of the ratings for two of those projects are shown in Figures 2.6 and 2.7. The ratings shown here are not necessarily definitive, although a certain degree of consistency was observed when different groups of students evaluated

	Client Success Indicators	Team Success Factors
Scope	75/95	40/60
Quality	75/95	30/40
Cost	20/90	8/40
Schedule	25/80	30/40
Risk		8/40
Integration		10/30
Reporting		5/30
Contract		20/40
Communication		15/50
Team	15/50	20/70
Client	30/90	10/30
Vendor		10/30
Overall	240/500	206/500

Figure 2.6 Project Evaluation, Example: Boston S.E. Expressway

	Client Success Indicators	Team Success Factors
Scope	75/95	40/60
Quality	75/95	30/40
Cost	20/90	20/40
Schedule	30/80	30/40
Risk		8/40
Integration		10/30
Reporting		20/30
Contract		15/40
Communication		40/50
Team	15/50	20/70
Client	30/90	20/30
Vendor		20/30
Overall	245/500	273/500

Figure 2.7 Project Evaluation, Example: English Channel Tunnel

the same project. Equally important, the explicit quantified indices provided a rational platform for debate and clarification. One interesting contrast between these two projects is that, although the client indices are roughly equal, indicating similar client satisfaction in these projects,

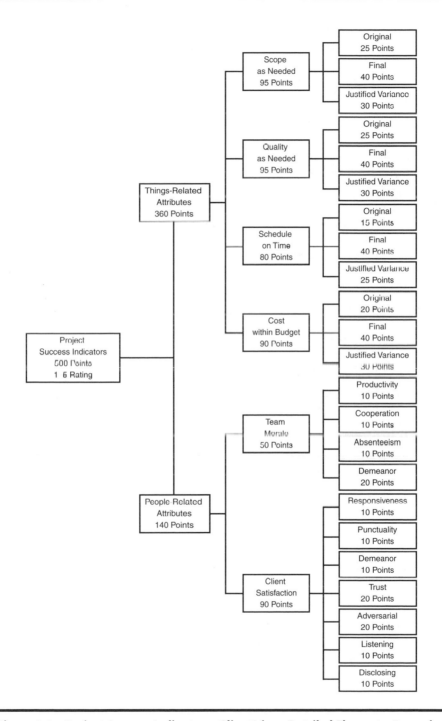

Figure 2.8   Project Success Indicators: Client View, Detailed Elements, Example, Including Weighting Criteria

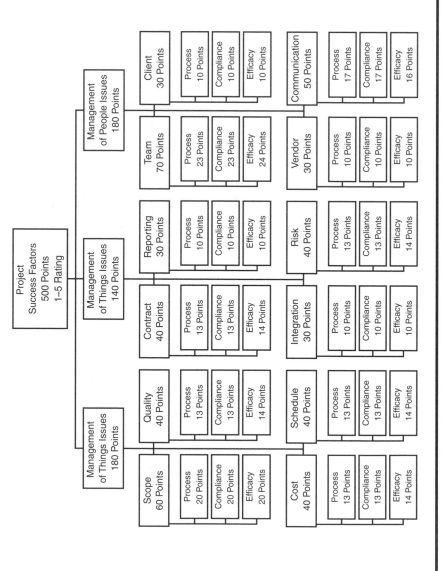

Figure 2.9   Project Success Factors: Team View, Detailed Elements, Example, Including Weighting Criteria

	Inception	Planning	Implement	Close-Out
Scope, 95	√	√	√	√
Quality, 95	√	√	√	√
Cost, 90	√	√	√	√
Schedule, 80	√	√	√	√
Team, 50	√	√	√	√
Client, 90	√	√	√	√
Overall Performance, 500	—	—	—	—

Figure 2.10 Life-Cycle Performance Matrix: Client Indicators

	Inception	Planning	Implement	Close-Out
Scope, 60	√	√	√	√
Quality, 40	√	√	√	√
Cost, 40	√	√	√	√
Schedule, 40	√	√	√	√
Contract, 40	√	√	√	√
Risk, 40	√	√	√	√
Integration, 30	√	√	√	√
Reporting, 30	√	√	√	√
Team, 70	√	√	√	√
Client, 30	√	√	√	√
Vendor, 30	√	√	√	√
Communication, 50	√	√	√	√
Overall Performance, 500	—	—	—	—

Figure 2.11 Life-Cycle Performance Matrix: Team Factors

the team indices are significantly dissimilar. All indications are that the project with a higher team rating was conducted in a more orderly fashion.

If a detailed success evaluation, beyond the structures shown earlier in this chapter, is desired, then any of the following enhancements can be applied to the models. First, the breakdown of the model can be extended to level three in order to rank more detailed features of the client and team success attributes (Figures 2.8 and 2.9). Second, instead of rating the entire project as a whole, one might rate the performance of the project in each of the life-cycle phases. And finally, one might assign different weights to the performance in each of the life-cycle phases (Figures 2.10 and 2.11).

CONCLUSIONS

Client and team viewpoints on project performance are fundamentally different. To recognize this difference while formalizing the process of evaluating the project, one can use the structures described in this chapter. For best results, the project must be rated and evaluated at regular and frequent intervals during the life of the project.

3

MARGINAL PROJECT
PERFORMANCE

3.1 OVERVIEW

The point at which an organization realizes that a project is out of control varies from organization to organization. This realization is directly related to the organizational sophistication in planning projects and persistence in monitoring project performance. Concern regarding the below-expectation performance of the project may be initiated by any of the stakeholders: the client, supporting organizations, accounting department, contracts office, project audit group, or any variation of the PMO that might exist in the organization. On rare occasions, the team members and/or the project manager might voice concerns regarding the health of the project.

An important evaluation, or self-evaluation, must be conducted at this juncture. The objective is not only to conduct a realistic determination of the progress of deliverables but also to perform a careful analysis of the causes of the mal-performance. Naturally, such an analysis must be devoid of emotions and internal politics in order to be useful. Although the list of possible reasons for mal-performance is almost limitless, the most common causes are fuzzy objectives and the resulting reactive style of managing project scope, risks, cost, schedule, and contracts. To a lesser extent, project failures or near-failures can have their roots in poor communication and unanticipated shortage of resources (Bullen and Rockart, 1981; Pinto and Slevin, 1987, 1988; Pinto and Prescott, 1988; Baily, 2000; Rad and Raghavan, 2000).

Formalized literature and anecdotal case data provide many examples of projects that were not recognized as runaway projects until very late in the project life. Although some attribute the late realization of a disaster situation to sinister motives, it is entirely possible that the cause for the bulk of these cases can be traced to misplaced optimism of an overly enthusiastic project team that continually ignored warning signs with hopes of reversing the undesirable course of the project, even after most of the allotted time and resources of the project have been spent on delivering a minority of the deliverables (Baily, 2000; Deloitte & Touche, 2000). Once the realization is made that it will cost far more than expected to deliver the desired product, or that the project is out of control, the organization will put remedial plans in place. The organization then will attempt to salvage something useful from the project. Usually, the project is not terminated until a few attempts have been made to remedy the mal-performance features of the project. Termination becomes necessary when the project is so far out of control that it cannot be managed, or if the resources are better used on other projects, or no additional funds are available for recovery, or if the delay is such that the product would be obsolete when and if it is ever delivered. Nevertheless, recovery must be done at the right time, so it is important to ensure that the project is at a point at which some elements can be salvaged and that the new delivery date is acceptable to the stakeholders.

As a testimonial to the adage that no one wants to be the bearer of bad news, the condition of the runaway project is often reported using euphemisms such as a bit off track, challenged, bears watching, is in the "yellow" zone, troubled, challenged, has excessive variance, excessive undesirable variance, negative float, negative funding surplus, and shortfall in project value. A more realistic, and admittedly harsher, set of descriptors would be runaway, in crisis, or out of control.

3.2 TWO TYPICAL RUNAWAY PROJECTS

In internal projects, the exchange currency is usually resource and time and not necessarily money. Thus, when a project is commissioned, the project manager is permitted to use a specified number of resources for a specific number of weeks or months. Then, if the project manager wishes to ask for an increase in project cost without changing the timeline, the project manager requests more resources. More commonly, the project manager asks for a collective increase in cost and duration. This modification is signaled by requesting to keep the current complement of resources for a certain period of time beyond the planned delivery date of the project. Thus, the request simply mentions an extension of time, and it is usually granted because generally more tolerance for variance is acceptable for an internal project.

Figure 3.1 shows the progress of a typical internal project. The project manager predicted that this project would be completed on time, and

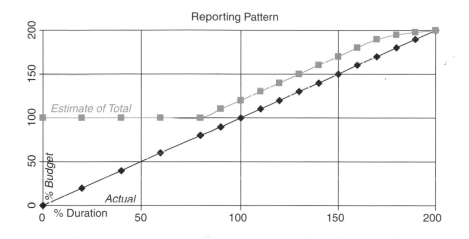

Figure 3.1   Traditional Cost Increase Request: Internal Project

hence on budget, for the first 80% of the project's schedule. Once 80% of the original time, and hence cost, of the project was consumed, then the project manager asked for a small extension of time, and hence budget, beyond the original baseline. From that point forward, the project manager continually postponed the delivery date by 1 week until the project was delivered at 200% of the original time, and hence at 200% of the original budget. It is an important point that, during the second half of the actual duration of the project, the project manager continually insisted that the project was only a few weeks from completion. It is a more important point that this behavior is not rooted in dishonesty and deception, but rather in optimism and wishful planning, albeit the optimism is grossly misplaced.

The second example deals with an external project that was conducted under a fixed-price contract. Usually, the incentive for engaging in fixed-price contracts is based on the common belief that the client will transfer the project risks to the contractor, while empowering the contractor to implement cost saving and efficiency measures in the performance of the project. If there are no unusual and unpredictable occurrences in the project environment, the project might in fact be conducted smoothly, thus resulting in the prompt delivery of the desired product to the client, while yielding an attractive profit to the contractor. As such, many clients do not keep a watchful eye on the performance of the contractors. Figure 3.2 shows the performance of a typical fixed-price contract. Although the contractor claimed, for the first 22 months of the 24-month contract, that the project was on target, suddenly at month 22–23, the contractor announced that the project was not going to be completed on time and within the original budget. The contractor

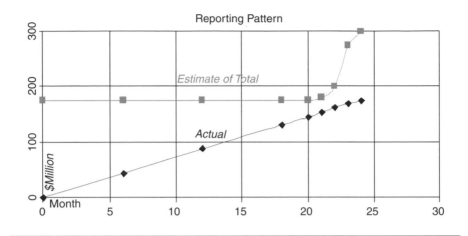

Figure 3.2   Another Cost Increase Example: Fixed-Price Contract

adjusted the cost and schedule overruns upward during the next two reporting cycles until the project was halted at month 24 with minimal delivery. The contractor requested additional funds and a time extension for the project even though the contract was of a fixed-price nature. The contractor claimed that the cost increase and schedule overrun were due to unusual conditions that were known to the client and not disclosed to the contractor in a timely fashion, and therefore the contract had to be amended. Without debating that particular aspect of the project, the point that is germane here is that the contractor did not discover the runaway nature of the project until some 90% of the project time had lapsed. Equally important, the client chose not to monitor the contractor's progress very closely, and therefore, was surprised by this cost increase revelation (Anonymous, 1997a,b).

Therefore, it is in the best interest of the client to conduct a close monitoring of the progress of all internal and external projects in order to provide an early, and a realistic, warning of the trouble signs of the project, and ultimately to ensure satisfactory completion of the project. A greater degree of success of projects not only will identify the organization as an enlightened and proactive one, but also will facilitate the achievement of organizational strategic goals and the attainment of higher profits. Three examples of high-profile public projects that suffered from various degrees of late discovery of project mal-performance are the Pit-9 project in Idaho, the Super-Conducting-Super-Collider project in Texas, and the SE Expressway project in Massachusetts (Rubin, 1991; Bowers, 1994; Anonymous, 1997a,b, 2001; Deloitte & Touche, 2000).

The literature on project performance generally concludes that there is a low rate of success for project across all industries. Figure 3.3 shows

```
■  16% Fully Successful
■  32% Partially Successful
■  52% Failed
```

Figure 3.3   Success Rate of Internal Projects

results of a typical study conducted by the Standish Group and posted to http://www.standishgroup.com/chaos.html. Figure 3.4 shows the reasons for failure of internal projects according to the same study (Rad and Raghavan, 2000). Although the elements are somewhat unique, the overall tone of the element composition in this study is somewhat common to most studies. The commonality is that scope definition is the most important element of project planning, and that lack of a clear scope usually contributes heavily to the runaway predicament of a project. Formal literature and anecdotal data indicate that an average project is expected to cost twice as much and take twice as long to complete, as compared to the original plans. It is an important point that the missions and activities and functions of a PMO directly speak to these issues and to the prevention of these causes of failure.

3.3 THE PROJECT AUDIT

Once the client, or the project manager, comes to the painful realization that a project is seriously late and over budget, the first order of business is an objective and clear determination of the status of the project through a detailed audit of the project. The audit needs to be completed quickly, generally in a 2- to 3-day time period, because usually at this point the runaway project is nearing the end of its life cycle.

This sequence of events is not necessarily universal. Sometimes a routine evaluation, such as the one described earlier in this book, will serve as the warning signal for the performance of the project. An

```
■  Incomplete Requirements
■  Lack of User Involvement
■  Lack of Resources
■  Unrealistic Expectations
■  Lack of Executive Support
■  Changing Specifications/Requirements
■  Lack of Planning
■  Product No Longer Needed
```

Figure 3.4   Why Internal Projects Fail

audit must specifically address explicit and detailed recitation of objectives and quantified delivery expectations in terms of scope, cost, schedule, constraints, and resources, as the recovery to follow must be done in the context of the project's objectives. Key items to examine are the WBS, project plan, identified risks, actual risks, rcsources, project schedule, changes requested and implemented, and management control processes. The focus of the audit is to determine the actual status of the project and then to determine how best to fix it. A self-assessment is difficult and typically not effective because it is difficult to be objective in the process of criticizing oneself. An external audit is recommended, with possible involvement of some of the project team members.

A charter for the audit team is recommended to detail its purpose and scope. The relationship of the audit team to the project team is critical and should be managed carefully. The purpose of the audit is not to serve as a "gotcha" tool or to blame specific project team members but instead to determine how best to recover the project. The project manager should view the audit as an essential tool to determine the course of action to follow in the recovery process.

The audit team then should thoroughly review key project documents with particular attention to the contract, statement of work or scope statement, the WBS, the project plan, cost, budget, and tracking systems. It is important to determine whether the WBS has been developed to a sufficient level of detail, or the scope of the project has been defined completely, so that each work package ends with a specific deliverable and there is adequate monitoring and control. The team also will conduct interviews with the client, sponsors, vendors, and members of the project team, as appropriate. As mentioned previously, what was done may be viewed differently by different project stakeholders.

The audit team should then prepare a report describing the scope of the audit, key findings, and recommendations. It is suggested that, in order to foster agreement on the next step to which to proceed, clear and concrete recommendations must be developed by the audit team. As a practical consideration, the number of these findings should be kept to less than 6. The project recovery team can effectively address 5 or 6 findings, but not 50 (Arter, 1994, p. 61). A small percentage of key characteristics will account for a high percentage of problems. Therefore, the audit must distinguish the "vital few from the trivial many." Each finding should be a clear, concise statement of a specific problem. The findings statement should be followed by a restatement of the control element that is in need of attention, and a list of the individual facts that support the findings statement. The findings thus prepared will become the basis for the project recovery plan.

3.4 RECOVERY PLANS

The purpose of the recovery plan is to chart a course that would lead to a successful project completion. Probably the most important part of the recovery plan is the development of a more accurate statement of the general goals for the project and a new set of triple constraints (Figure 3.5). With results of a detailed audit in hand, a realistic course of action is then charted for the project completion. The modified execution plans should also include details of project management procedures and tools that will be used during the remainder of the project. Thus, modified scope definition, budget, schedule, and resource demands will be developed for the project. Naturally, these details need not be developed from scratch, because one can take advantage of all the original planning data, and the project experience to date, in developing the recovery plan; however, the recovery plans must be developed without any undue emphasis on the original baseline values. In most cases work on the project will continue during this time of recovery planning; therefore, it may be appropriate for professionals who are outside of the project team to prepare the recovery plan.

The enhanced baseline and the recovery plans will include new performance targets for scope, quality, cost, and schedule; updated management expectations; more rigorous monitoring and reporting; and current resource constraints. Documents should be modified in the light of current earned value (Figure 3.5). The key difference here, compared to the original project plan, is that this recovery plan should be one that cannot fail. The next step, and this is a sobering step for all stakeholders, is to announce, publish, and approve the modified baseline for the project. Having done that, the project would then execute the recovery plan and proceed on its new course, hopefully toward a satisfactory completion.

Polished project management skills are essential here. Almost all projects have milestones whose primary purpose is to validate and verify

```
■ Formulate New Performance Targets for
    ■ Scope
    ■ Quality
    ■ Cost
    ■ Schedule
■ Modify the Baseline in the Light of
    ■ Current Earned Value
    ■ Management Expectations
    ■ Resource Constraints
```

Figure 3.5   Develop Enhanced Baseline

the progress pace of the project and to put the stakeholders at ease with respect to the pace of the attainment of project objectives. This issue will be more crucial with projects that are on a recovery path, because if the recovery plans begin to falter, then project cancellation becomes a realistic option, and one that may be executed very quickly. All stakeholders must be involved, and at the first indication of any serious difficulties after this point, they must be informed immediately.

3.5 THE ROLE OF THE PMO

More often than not, it is during the recovery phase of a critical project that an organization examines the wisdom of establishing a PMO so that expensive and time-consuming recoveries will become rare. Sometimes, the organization might choose to provide the PMO functionality only for this project. This organizational entity is an abbreviated form of a comprehensive PMO, and it is often referred to as the Project Office. In other cases, organizations authorize a Project Office for every project that is initiated, but they stop short of authorizing a permanent organizational PMO. By definition, a Project Office is dissolved once the project is completed. As such, this office provides some of the beneficial services of a PMO to the project at hand without extending such good practices beyond the bounds of the project. By virtue of its missions and objectives, a Project Office takes on a role that is somewhat reactive rather than forward looking and proactive. Again, the advantage of a PMO is that the organization can capitalize on the project experiences of previous projects. Such benefits will be minimized if the Project Office is treated as a remedial quick-fix unit, and if the data collection and information dissemination are treated as temporary ventures.

A Project Office will develop formalized processes and procedures for management of project activities in things- and people-related areas, albeit these procedures are nonstandard, one time, and probably nonuniform. The Project Office's assistance in things-related areas includes managing scope, quality, cost, schedule, risk, reporting, contracts, integration, and environmental change of the project. In people-related areas, the Project Office will assist with managing communications, team morale, vendor relations, and the all-important client relations.

Quite often, the realignment of runaway projects must be done with extreme haste. Thus, there may be insufficient time to train the project manager and the project team. The rationale is that benefits of a training session will be realized after 1 or 2 weeks, during which time a portion of the project team will be out of commission. Notwithstanding that drawback, if there is sufficient time, in order to enhance the competence of project personnel, the Project Management Office will conduct training

	Consult	Mentor	Augment
Scope	—	—	—
Quality	—	—	—
Cost	—	—	—
Schedule	—	—	—
Risk	—	—	—
Integration	—	—	—
Reporting	—	—	—
Contract	—	—	—
Environmental	—	—	—
Communication	—	—	—
Team	—	—	—
Client	—	—	—
Vendor	—	—	—

Figure 3.6   PMO Recovery Functions

for the project team. Training is provided in all fundamentals of project management for everyone, with specific concentrations for selected team members. Otherwise, and more commonly, consulting, mentoring, or even augmenting for project personnel on an as-needed basis will be implemented to meet the immediate objectives of the team (Figure 3.6). Then, on a case-by-case basis, the subject matter might include planning, estimating, scheduling, scope management, and the like. Often, proper application of project management software is included in the subject of such knowledge transfer.

The PMO formalizes the process of training, consulting, mentoring, and augmenting for the recovering projects. The process starts with efforts to identify the competencies that are necessary for each project management function within the project at hand. Using such information, targeted individuals receive the assistance necessary to perform their project functions. It is an important point that the objective is not to improve the general competency of the team members, but rather to give the team members whatever skills they need in order to complete the current project as expeditiously as possible (Figure 3.7).

In some situations, the project manager and team may be unable to execute the recovery plan. The PMO then may need to appoint a project recovery manager. Leading such a task can be a thankless job for many people, given all the problems that need to be corrected and the risk of potential failure. The recovery manager should be someone who has previous experience in similar projects and also has leadership skills to motivate the team, work with stakeholders, make decisions, and hold the

- Project Manager
  - All Project Management Areas, Rigorous
- Team
  - Basics
    - All Areas of Things Management
    - Selected Areas of the Technical Specialty of the Project
  - Rigorous
    - Most Areas of People Management
    - Selected Areas of Things Management
    - Selected Areas of the Technical Specialty of the Project

Figure 3.7   Training

team accountable for the project's goals. Ideally, the recovery manager should review the audit findings and help prepare the recovery plan. On a regular basis, he or she must focus on reviewing progress and on assessing future risk.

At this point, everyone will be concerned about the project's progress, given the events to date. Therefore, a key task will be to reach out and communicate with project stakeholders and provide regular updates of progress to management and the customers. Customer relationship management is essential in such a crisis atmosphere. The recovery manager should address key customer issues without becoming defensive. This is not the time to "over promise"; instead, the customer must be given realistic expectations as to what is possible in the current situation. Accordingly, the recovery manager must be proficient in applying a wide variety of sophisticated interpersonal skills, especially in terms of resolving conflict and also in rebuilding team morale (Flannes and Levin, 2001, pp. 364–368).

The PMO also will foster a commitment to continuous improvement. This is a key ingredient for project management maturity at higher levels in that the PMO can identify lessons learned and archive them in a repository for use by other ongoing and future projects to avoid thing- and people-related mistakes encountered again by troubled projects.

From an organizational viewpoint, project recovery is essentially similar to redoing tasks on the assembly line. As such, this experience carries the significant losses involved in redoing any production task. A harmful side effect of rework is its detrimental impact on the team morale, not to mention the detrimental effects on the overall cost and schedule. As has been demonstrated in the case of physical quality of products, the cost of doing things right the first time is always less than the cost of redoing things. For projects, this concept applies on a grand scale.

CONCLUSIONS

A typical project is likely to be completed at twice its original budget and at twice its originally anticipated duration. Projects should be audited on a regular basis to isolate problem areas and to develop plans to bring the mal performing projects into an acceptable state. If a project is significantly out of line from the anticipated progress, then formal recovery plans must be devised. The project must be re-initiated with a set of realistic plans. The PMO can assist the recovery plans by providing consultation, mentoring, or even augmenting the project staff.

4

PROJECT MANAGER COMPETENCY

4.1 OVERVIEW

The term *competent* means that the project manager or team member is operating at acceptable levels of performance in his or her areas of training and experience; *competence* does not mean that the project manager has perfect knowledge of all areas. Moreover, competence involves the ability to assess personal strengths and then to sharpen one's skills in those areas that require skill improvements. Competence also involves knowing what you don't know, and having the courage to express concerns about these potential deficiencies and obtain assistance and expertise when needed. Boyatzis (1982) explains that competency is a term that is widely used but has come to mean different things to different people. It is generally accepted that competency encompasses knowledge, skills, attitudes, and behaviors that are causally related to superior job performance. In other words, competent people are capable people.

Frame (1999) states that the issue of competence is one of the two or three most significant issues facing organizations today. He notes that a competent project manager, along with a competent team and a supportive organization, are ingredients for success because they produce intended results. Interest in competence in project management is based on the reasonable and widely held assumption that if people who manage and work on projects are competent, they will perform effectively, and this will then in turn lead to successful projects and successful organizations.

Competence is important beecause of the major variations in the ability of project participants to do their jobs. In the past, getting by was good enough. Today, getting by is a prescription for failure. Individuals must strive to be superlative. The practices of the project manager are at the heart of any successful project. Further, repeated success of projects results from good processes, and from project managers who continue to learn and improve their personal practices. To work toward a personal improvement program in project management, the first step is to establish a baseline of knowledge, skills, and competencies. Humphrey (1989) uses the following metaphor for competency: if you don't know where you are, a map won't help. The existence of this baseline will allow the organization to recognize whether or not performance is improving. The baseline will also serve as the framework for a personal improvement program, and it will enable a person to measure specific improvements in his/her professional profile.

Although the proactive task of increasing project management competency can be undertaken independent of a PMO, the effectiveness of a competent cadre of project managers can be magnified significantly if these project managers have the full suite of PMO services at their disposal. The PMO can methodically identify the project management competencies that are necessary for the project manager and for each project team member. On the basis of this competency plan, the PMO will develop a project position matrix relating the knowledge areas to the organizational position that would perform certain project management tasks. The determination of the desired competencies of project managers is highly influenced by organizational needs, strategies, and culture. When a formalized PMO is fully implemented, such determination can be made effectively and systematically. The overall organizational plans for project management competency development would also include identification of organizational changes that are necessary to sustain effective project management. These organizational changes include efforts to recognize project management as a profession with a distinct job classification and with a bona fide career path. Thus, formalized project manager position descriptions and career tracks must be identified. The result is a family of positions in the project management field, enabling people to enhance career opportunities, and thus providing the organization with a knowledgeable base of employees exhibiting and demonstrating project management skills, abilities, and experience.

One of the more common techniques in determining the desired project management competency is to identify the successful project managers in the organization to use as a first approximation of the competency model. To the extent possible and practicable, attempts should be made to determine what critical skills facilitated the success of particular managers and how these skills were acquired. Care should be taken not to identify those project managers who simply appear to be successful but rather to identify those who have managed projects that have been deemed to be successful based on the indices developed earlier in this book. One important additional feature of this exercise is to determine what additional skills would have been necessary to produce an even higher level of success for the project. Therefore, clear and specific criteria to measure success are required. With the backdrop provided by this information, one then would highlight the project management skills that the future successful project managers need. It would be highly useful if these skills were prioritized consistent with organizational objectives and goals. One then can establish organizational standards for junior project managers, intermediate level managers, and senior project managers. Each successive level would include the knowledge and skills from the previous level(s). Another approach to determining the desired project management competency is to develop a prioritized list of between seven and ten activities that occupy a project manager's time. This list then is reconciled with another list consisting of between seven to ten tasks that are, or should be, the responsibility of a project manager. This exercise would require a focus group of experienced project managers.

4.2 DIFFERENT SKILL SETS

Ideally, the project manager should be treated like the CEO of a small enterprise. As such, the project manager must possess a broad range of knowledge and skills in the technical area of the project, in things management, in people management, and in supporting areas such as marketing, finance, and organizational behavior.

During the early evolution periods of project management, competence in the technical area of specialty of the project was the only requirement for the position of project manager. This heavy emphasis on the technical area of specialty still exists in some organizations that treat project management as a subset of the technical disciplines. Thus, a project manager makes a professional transition to the discipline of project management by way of another knowledge domain, entering project management through experience and mastery of process. Unfortunately, anyone may use the title of project manager, with no required proof of competence and no formal training. Looking carefully at job descriptions of project managers in some organizations, one might notice that a large majority of the required competencies are those of the technical discipline, and that a small fraction of the required competencies refer to project management skills. Figures 4.1 and 4.2 are very close paraphrased recitations of published advertisements for professional positions. The interesting point is that only one, and the last one at that, of the job skills deals with project management, and yet the title of the positions is clearly project manager.

- Sendmail Administration
- Solaris UNIX Administration
- DNS Management (BIND version)
- WAN and Architecture
- Cisco Router and Switch Configuration
- BGP and NAT
- Firewalls (preferably Cisco PIX and Checkpoint Firewall-1)
- Network Security Concepts and Policy
- Intrusion Detection Systems (prefer RealSecure by ISS)
- PERL, UNIX shell scripting, Visual Basic, and C
- Project Management

Figure 4.1 IT Project Manager Skills

- Environmental Engineering, with Experience in
  - Solid Waste
  - Groundwater
  - Numerical Modeling of
    - Environmental Systems
    - Air Pollution Control
- Electrical Engineering
- Digital Signal Processing
- Computer Applications in Engineering
- Thermodynamics or Fluid Mechanics
- Engineering Mechanics
- Engineering Materials
- Project Management

Figure 4.2 Engineering Project Manager Skills

Skills in managing the quantitative areas of the project became the major emphasis of project management competencies during the next stage of evolution of the project management profession. These areas cover issues such as cost management, schedule management, records management, quality control, scope management, contract management, configuration management, etc.

There is no question that quantitative and technical issues must be addressed as part of the planning and execution of a project. However, as became apparent during the ensuing maturity phases of the project management profession, these knowledge areas are necessary but not sufficient on their own for the success of a project. It was discovered that sometimes project performance falls short of expectations even though

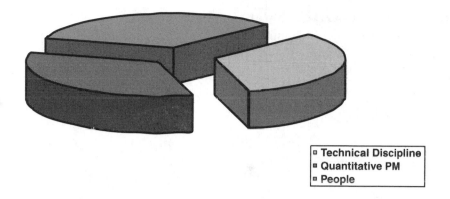

Figure 4.3   Project Management Skills

the quantitative aspects of the project are addressed as part of planning and implementation. Such mal-performances occur when all the quantitative characteristics of a project are planned and implemented with little attention to the needs, traits, and behavior of the people who ultimately implement the project. This observation led to the formalization of the process by which people-issues are addressed as part of project planning and implementation. The areas of emphasis thus added cover issues such as personality profiles, team building, team charter, conflict management, communications management, negotiations, and people's reaction to organizational changes.

There is an ongoing debate among project managers as to whether qualitative issues are more important than quantitative issues within the context of the success of a project. It is fair to say that both are important and necessary, and that omission of any portion of either one of these areas will detract from the success of the project. Agreeing that one needs all of the above, it is necessary to develop plans to deliver such competencies (Figure 4.3). For the purposes of visualization, the competencies important to, and useful in, project management can be divided into two major categories: things and people, and will be treated as such in the next section (Figure 4.4).

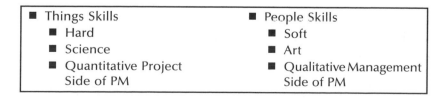

Figure 4.4   Categorization of Project Management Skills

4.3 THINGS-RELATED SKILLS

The category of things-related skills is referred to as hard skills, the science side of project management, and managing things. This category includes the skills for dealing with quantitative facets of the project, which are usually inanimate, but lend themselves to extensive analysis, tabulation, and quantitative analysis. The quantitative elements of project management were the first areas to be used, to be developed, and to reach maturity. These skill areas are most commonly those that produce charts, create tables, develop lists, and design administrative forms. These skill areas include project selection schemas and formalized techniques for planning, estimating, and scheduling. These areas also include change management policies, risk management procedures, project monitoring and control procedures, contract management policies, and project documentation. Figure 4.5 shows a partial list of project managerial skills and duties that fall in the things category.

■ Plan	■ Define Metrics
■ Develop WBS	■ Determine Earned Value
■ Schedule	■ Suggest Decision Tools
■ Estimate	■ Promote Risk Management
■ Prepare Gantt Charts	■ Issue Status Reports
■ Formulate Network Diagrams	■ Conduct Resource Estimating
■ Establish Monitoring Standards	■ Perform Resource Leveling
■ Conduct Variance Analysis	■ Conduct Network Compression

Figure 4.5 Things Skills and Duties

4.4 PEOPLE-RELATED SKILLS

Project Management Institute in its *The Future of Project Management* (1999) noted that the "people side of project management is getting more complex" (p. xiii). It states that many rate capability in people skills as more important than leadership or management skills and far more important than industry expertise and technical skills (p. xv).

Projects rarely fail because of technology, but they often fail because of people. The people side of projects has been referred to as the soft-sciences side of projects, the qualitative side, or the side of projects that is an art and not a science. This category includes the skills for dealing with the qualitative facets of the project, which usually involve humans, and they do not readily and easily lend themselves to extensive analysis, tabulation, and quantitative analysis. The general emphasis of this series

■ Communications	■ Flexibility
■ Teamwork	■ Negotiation
■ Conflict Resolution	■ Client Relations
■ Trust	■ Mentoring
■ Honesty	■ Consulting
■ Sociability	■ Training
■ Integrity	■ Leadership
	■ Staff Development

Figure 4.6   People Skills and Duties

of activities includes the skill set that is necessary to deal with other people. Examples of such skills are proper communication, team building, conflict management, good supervision, internal and external alliances and relationship building with stakeholders, working with others to generate creative ideas and solutions, participatory management, and performance evaluation. Figure 4.6 shows a partial list of project managerial skills and duties that fall in the people category.

4.5 ORGANIZATION-RELATED ISSUES

As the organization becomes more enlightened, and as the importance of effective project management becomes more widely acknowledged, additional measures can be implemented to integrate project management culture into the organization. Crawford (1999) identifies issues to consider when assessing project management competence and how standards play a part in this process. Her research uncovers some interesting elements of the project management community, and begins to put some of the current project management practices into the context of where we need to focus our attention for the future of this profession. She argues that the standards should be used as a basis for assessing and developing competence, but that project managers also need skills in such areas as the ability to interpret project environment factors to create successful project outcomes.

Thus, an emerging area of emphasis in project management competencies includes organizational planning skills and full understanding of the behavior of a multitude of projects within an organization. These areas cover issues such as support of projects within organizations, managing contributions of various divisions to organizational project goals, promoting enterprise consistency of project management procedures, measuring overall success of divisional projects, generating interest to sell products and services to current and potential customers, ensuring that project strategies are aligned with organizational goals, establishing infrastructures

> ■ Support of Projects within Organizations
> ■ Contributions of Divisions to Projects
> ■ Enterprise Consistency of Procedures
> ■ Degree of Success of Divisional Projects
> ■ Generating Interest in Customers for Services
> ■ Alignment of Project Strategies with Organizational Goals
> ■ Conduct Assessments Using Maturity Models
> ■ Enhanced Procedures for Project Selection

Figure 4.7 Organizational Issues in Planning

that support project environments, using maturity models, conducting assessments of the organizational maturity, evaluating the sophistication of an organization in fostering successful projects, developing project selection models, and managing project portfolios (Figure 4.7).

As an example, Gadeken (1994), in research conducted for the Department of Defense, identified six competencies that distinguish outstanding project managers from their contemporaries.

1. A sense of ownership and mission — The project manager sees himself or herself as responsible for the project and is able to articulate problems or issues from a broader organizational or mission perspective.
2. Political awareness — The project manager has identified the influential stakeholders, both inside and outside the organization, recognizes and understands their requirements, and has determined how best to work with them.
3. Develops relationships — The project manager spends time and energy getting to know sponsors, users, and suppliers.
4. Fosters a strategic influence — The project manager builds coalitions and orchestrates situations to overcome obstacles and obtain support.
5. Performs interpersonal assessments — The project manager identifies specific interests, motivations, strengths, and weaknesses of project team members.
6. Has an action orientation — The project manager is proactive and reacts to problems energetically and with a sense of urgency.

These competencies fall almost exclusively within the category of managing the external environment or the relationships outside the project. Gadeken's study concluded that technical expertise is not the most important requirement for successful project management. Gadeken notes that the transition from functional specialist to project manager may be conceptually quite difficult because a project manager needs external interface skills far more than other types. The premise is that projects will be more assured of success if they are implemented within an organization whose culture and attitude foster the project mentality, and whose reward structure recognizes project managers who consistently complete successful projects.

As organizations base more of their futures on complex projects, their need for more predictable projects increases, again affirming a need for more competent project managers. The skills listed here relate to project management, although not all project managers need be versed in these skills. More experienced project managers who are assigned to the PMO typically are the only ones who need these skills to handle the organizational-related project management functions.

4.6 COMPETENCY ANALYSIS

Probably because of the diversity of the multitude of duties and responsibilities of a project manager, many organizations do not have standard job descriptions for this important position. If job descriptions do in fact exist, they tend to emphasize specific deliverables rather than the skills that are needed to actually achieve and produce these deliverables. The title of project manager also has different meanings in different organizations.

Given that the PMO would have the full perspective of the organizational goals and resource characteristics, and organizational career path intricacies, the PMO would be in a good position to develop a list of several grades of project management positions. The PMO would then draft job descriptions of the duties and responsibilities of each of these grades. Finally, these descriptions will include the specific project management skills that are needed for a masterful execution of these duties. These skills can be categorized under things and people (see Figure 4.8).

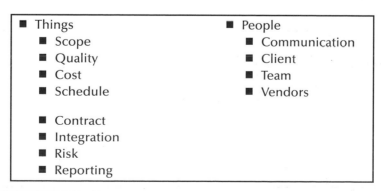

Figure 4.8   Project Management Facets

Most common indicators of competence are experience and credentials. Experience can be in all areas of knowledge, in one area of knowledge, in one discipline, or in several industries. The most common project management credentials are publications in any of the knowledge areas, courses in these skill areas, college degrees in project management, and project management certification (see Appendix A for a brief overview of five professional association certification programs).

With these required skill descriptions in hand, one can very quickly determine the skills necessary for each member of the project team for a newly commissioned project (Figure 4.9). Under ideal circumstances, all project management personnel of the organization meet or surpass these requirements; that would be an organization that earns the highest possible project management maturity rating, a level five. If the organization and its employees have not reached this stage of maturity yet, then it is likely that some of the prospective team members might not possess the desired project management competencies to the extent necessary for execution of the forthcoming project. In such cases, the PMO will provide assistance to the project manager and to the project team in dealing with difficult situations. Again, depending on the circumstances, the assistance will be in the form of mentoring, consulting, or augmenting. The PMO also will provide the team members the benefit of a clearinghouse of best practices.

■ Identify the project management competencies necessary for each project management function.
■ Develop a project position matrix for knowledge, skills, and competency analysis.

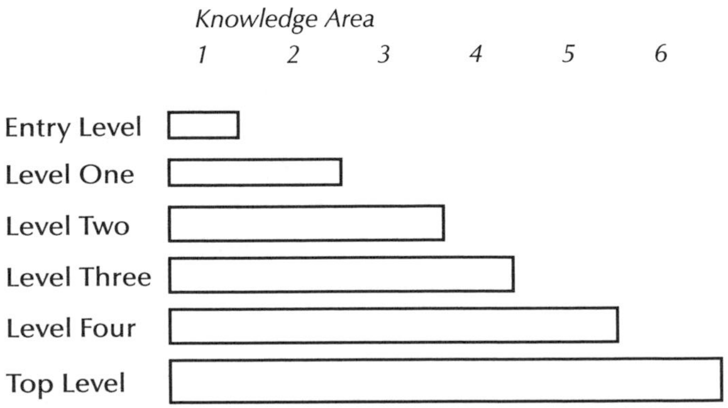

Knowledge Area

1   2   3   4   5   6

Entry Level
Level One
Level Two
Level Three
Level Four
Top Level

Figure 4.9   Competency Analysis

Recognizing the importance of this area, in 1998 Project Management Institute sponsored a Project Management Competency project to produce a competency *Framework* for the development of project managers. Project Management Institute published an exposure draft of this *Framework* in October 2001. Developed to provide guidance to both individuals and organizations as to how to manage the professional growth of the project manager, it is based on the premise that competencies directly affect performance. It is based on the nine knowledge areas and five processes (referred to as competency clusters), as defined in *A Guide to the Project Management Body of Knowledge, PMBOK® Guide, 2000 Edition*. It presents specific elements by competency cluster and related performance criteria. Self-assessment guidelines in terms of knowledge and performance competencies also are included. The *Framework* also presents personal competencies or personal characteristics underlying a person's capability to manage a project organized in six areas (Project Management Institute, 2001).

4.7 COMPETENCY TABLES

The PMO is in a good position to develop a competency model to determine the knowledge, skills, abilities, and the degree of proficiency in each competency that the employee is expected to exhibit at each job level. Such models could be built based on recent work completed by Project Management Institute (2001), tailoring it to meet the unique needs of the organization. Alternately, the PMO could develop a listing of project management positions, highlighting their duties, responsibilities, and competencies. Appendix 4B provides a listing of the duties of project-related personnel. Appendix 4C extends Appendix 4B by providing a listing of the competencies expected from the personnel who occupy those positions. These tables are based on the 39 processes in Project Management Institute's *PMBOK® Guide* (2000).

These tables complement the recent work done by Project Management Institute and can be used in conjunction with its competency *Framework*. Both these tables and Project Management Institute's competency *Framework* follow the *PMBOK® Guide* processes. However, the tables in these appendices describe specific project management positions, and a somewhat detailed description of their duties, while the Project Management Institute competency *Framework* focuses on generic performance criteria for each *PMBOK® Guide* process with examples of self-assessment guidelines. By using the tables in this book, one will recognize the specific behaviors, knowledge, and abilities that are required for each project management position. The tables also can be used to identify both short- and long-term mentoring or training needs.

The tables present project management positions that are characterized as project focused and enterprise oriented in the following fashion:

Project-Focused Positions

■ Project Team Member
■ Associate Project Manager
■ Project Manager

Enterprise-Oriented Positions

■ PMO Staff Member
■ Director, PMO
■ Vice President of Projects

These positions are defined as follows:

Project Team Member — Supports projects; spends 50 to 100% of his or her time working on projects; has some basic knowledge of project management and has taken some introductory courses in this area; may serve as a team leader, participates in medium and large projects, and may lead a small project; receives mentoring from the project manager and the PMO staff on specific tasks.

Associate Project Manager — Supports projects; spends 75 to 100% of his or her time working on projects; has served as a project team member; has knowledge of project management and has taken specific training emphasizing tools and techniques to use.

Project Manager — Leads projects of various sizes; spends 100% of his or her time working on projects; has taken training in project management; and has received project management certification.

PMO Staff Member — Supports the PMO; spends 100% of his or her time on project management; has served as a project team member; has previously managed small projects and possibly has served as a project control officer, and has knowledge of project management and has taken training in it; has or is working toward project management certification.

Director, PMO — Leads the PMO; spends 100% of his or her time on project management; has managed large, complex projects successfully; has taken advanced training in project management; and has obtained PM certification.

Vice President of Projects — Sponsors the PMO; spends 100% of his or her time on project management; has managed large, complex projects successfully; may have led the PMO; has taken advanced training in project management and has obtained project management certification; and contributes to the advancement of the profession.

4.8 ENHANCED COMPETENCY ANALYSIS

The tables in Appendices 4B and 4C should be used as a first approximation and not as a definitive and rigid checklist. As circumstances warrant, the tables should be modified and/or augmented in light of organizational characteristics. For example, they could be extended further to determine the specific competencies and the degree of proficiency on each competency required for a specific project. Then, with knowledge of the available individuals in the organization, the PMO could effectively match employees to projects. With the competency model and knowledge of available resources, the PMO could help identify short- and long-term training needs by showing the specific knowledge, skills, and abilities necessary for success at each level in project management. The PMO further could develop a proficiency chart to be used with the competency model to determine the appropriate competency level for each individual and to determine an individual's potential advancement to the next position in the project management career path.

This chart would benefit each person working in the field. He or she would then have available a clear set of expectations as to what is required for people working in project management. It would enable each person to determine whether or not they were ready to advance to the next level to develop a personal improvement strategy. This self-assessment is required because, to be more effective with others, it is essential to be more effective with oneself.

Organizations need to know how to recognize and select project managers, and how to continue to improve their project skills. As part of the overall organizational goals, the PMO would offer a continual training program for project managers and project team members. The training curriculum would then become the foundation upon which to establish a career path for project professionals. These training sessions will be orderly and will cover all core and supporting areas of project management. Given that, under ideal or desired circumstances, project management professionals are not hurried to take these training modules, they will be able to digest the material and relate it to their actual work, thereby receiving the most optimized educational benefit from such training.

There is no question that technical competency in the technical area of the project is an exceptionally important part of the team's professional attributes. Therefore, an additional level of competency enhancement can be provided for the team members by way of training and refreshers in the technical area of the project. Recognizing that this competency is necessary, although not sufficient, for the success of the project, training in technical subject matters can be scheduled either before or after all of the project management topics have been addressed but certainly not instead of project management topics.

Finally, the PMO would reassess the situation regularly with respect to needs and the available resource pool. Such a reassessment would come primarily from the resource requirements and size and complexity of the projects that are slated to start in the near future. The second component is the assessment of how successful team members are in handling project issues. Such an assessment will come from detailed project evaluations for the projects that these personnel have supported. Reconciling the requirements of the forthcoming projects with the characteristics of the prospective team members, the PMO can design an assistance plan specifically for that project. Again, the goal of a PMO should be to improve the overall competency of the organization in order that such assistance programs would not be necessary. Proactive selection and training of good project team members should eventually obviate the need for consulting, mentoring, and augmenting.

CONCLUSIONS

Ensuring that those who manage projects have the appropriate skills is the most direct and effective means of achieving success for the projects of the enterprise. Project managers should be competent in most or all of the details of the technical area of the project, things- and people-related issues of the project, and organization-related issues. A formalized and organization-specific procedure for assessing the competency of project managers and members of the project team must be established. Although such a procedure would require a nearly comprehensive knowledge for project managers, project team members would be required to acquire competency only in those areas that directly or indirectly impact their project functions.

APPENDIX 4A
CERTIFICATION PROGRAMS
IN PROJECT MANAGEMENT

4A.1 PROJECT MANAGEMENT INSTITUTE

Project Management Institute (PMI) has a certification program known as the Project Management Professional (PMP®), which is designed to objectively assess and measure professional knowledge. Candidates must demonstrate a level of experience and knowledge before being tested by means of a 4-hour multiple-choice exam. Recently, this process has been enhanced by an ongoing requirement to show commitment and involvement in the project management profession by obtaining Professional Development Units (PDUs), which are gained through contribution to the professional community, attendance at courses and seminars, and so on.

4A.2 ASSOCIATION FOR THE ADVANCEMENT
OF COST ENGINEERING

Certification indicates demonstrable expertise in the most current skills and knowledge of the profession. Individuals designated as Certified Cost Engineers (CCE®) or Certified Cost Consultants (CCC®) are recognized as having capabilities detailed within the definition of cost engineering. Certification in these areas is rapidly becoming the industry standard. Further, Association for the Advancement of Cost Engineering (AACE) requires recertification every 3 years, allowing the individual to demonstrate that he or she has maintained his or her expertise through work experience, continuing education, professional development, and active involvement in the profession. AACE's Certification Program encompasses specialties in cost estimating, cost control, business planning and management science, profitability analysis, project management, planning and scheduling, and other cost management specialties.

4A.3 ASSOCIATION FOR PROJECT MANAGEMENT

Association for Project Management (APM) has established a Certificated Project Manager (CPM) to provide peer recognition of competence in project management. To obtain the CPM, one must be a member of APM and must be managing or have managed a project or subproject. APM has four levels of projects:

- Level 1 — In-house with a single disciplinary team
- Level 2 — In-house with a multidisciplinary team
- Level 3 — Multi-company with a multidisciplinary team
- Level 4 — Multi-country, multi-company with a multidisciplinary team

Candidates complete a self-assessment concerning their knowledge of the key elements of project management. Candidates submit a project report, which then is followed by an interview with two assessors.

4A.4 AUSTRALIAN INSTITUTE OF PROJECT MANAGEMENT

Australian Institute of Project Management (AIPM) has three levels of certification:

- Qualified project practitioner
- Registered project manager
- Master project director

These levels of certification correspond to the Australian Quality Framework standards AQF4, AQF5, and AQF6. The certification process involves assessing both what a project manager knows as well as what he or she does, by use of a body of evidence to show an assessor the application of project management knowledge and skill.

4A.5 INTERNATIONAL PROJECT MANAGEMENT ASSOCIATION

International Project Management Association (IPMA) developed four levels of certification in its Competence Baseline:

- Project management practitioner
- Project management professional
- Project manager
- Projects director

It serves as the basis for all certification programs of the national associations and their certification bodies that are validated by IPMA.

APPENDIX 4B
DUTIES PERFORMED
BY PROJECT-RELATED
POSITIONS

Process/Position	Project Team Member	Associate Project Manager	Project Manager	PMO Staff Member	PMO Director	Vice President of Projects
Project Plan Development	Supports the preparation of the plan and its base documents (e.g., WBS, network diagram, risk management plan, cost estimates, etc.) and provides technical area specific inputs	Sets up the PMIS for use on the project Reviews historical information about previous projects for use in preparing the project plan Supports the preparation of the project plan and its base documents Maintains the plan as part of the project's documentation management system	Finalizes the project plan and issues it according to the communications management plan Involves stakeholders in project planning sessions Identifies constraints and assumptions affecting the project Reviews the project management methodology to determine if a scaled version should be used on the specific project	Assists in the development of the organization's project management methodology Assists in the development of a PMIS for all projects in the organization	Establishes a project management methodology for use throughout the organization Establishes guidelines for use of the methodology, including scalability to support different types of projects Establishes a PMIS for use by all projects Reviews project plans to ensure they are consistent with the organization's project management methodology	Reviews project plans to ensure that they support the organization's long-term strategy and business values Establishes organizational policies

Project Plan Execution					
Provides technical input to support project execution	Uses earned value management to integrate scope, schedule, and resources, and to measure and report project performance	Takes preventive and corrective action, as required	Provides support to status review meetings	Establishes requirements for a work authorization system for projects as part of the project management methodology	Ensures project work results support business objectives
Completes assigned work packages	Maintains the PMIS	Leads the team in completing the project	Assists in the development of an issues management system and maintains the system	Supports the project manager in obtaining needed product-specific resources to support the project	Ensures project strategies complement organizational goals
Attends and supports status review meetings	Reviews organizational procedures to ensure compliance on the project	Ensures that the team has access to required product skills and knowledge		Attends and participates in project status review meetings	Ensures that project management is an integral part of the organization's culture
Identifies needed changes and prepares change requests	Provides support to status review meetings	Communicates with stakeholders inside and outside of the organization concerning the project			Positions project management as a solution to the organization's problems
Assesses performance of work packages against the plan	Monitors performance against the project baseline	Conducts status review meetings			Serves as a public relations executive for project management
Keeps the project manager informed and up to date about progress	Establishes a work authorization system to support the project	Reviews work results			
Prepares work-related procedures	Establishes a documentation management system for the project	Identifies issues affecting the project and assigns action items as appropriate			
	Maintains project documentation	Provides authorization to team members to begin work on specific work packages			

Process/Position	Project Team Member	Associate Project Manager	Project Manager	PMO Staff Member	PMO Director	Vice President of Projects
Integrated Change Control	Identifies required changes and analyzes them for technical input	Maintains project baselines Supports the development of an integrated change control system for the project, including procedures for a Change Control Board as appropriate Reviews performance reports to assess issues that may cause future problems Maintains the PMIS Conducts a lessons learned meeting at the beginning of the project to establish a process to ensure that lessons learned are collected and analyzed	Establishes an integrated change control system for the project Approves changes to the project and incorporates them into a revised project baseline Determines whether a Change Control Board should be established Issues revised project plans as a result of changes Identifies, analyzes and reports lessons learned to the knowledge management system	Assists in the development of an integrated change control system and maintains the system Assists in the development of a knowledge management system and maintains the system	Establishes an integrated change control system for projects in the organization, including a classification system for project changes Establishes a knowledge management system for lessons learned on projects Uses data from the knowledge management system for continuous improvement of project management practices	Uses data from the knowledge management system for changes as required to overall organizational strategies and policies Adjusts project priorities in light of changing conditions affecting the organization

Initiation					
Provides input to the preparation of the product description Recommends potential projects for project selection	Recommends potential projects for project selection	Recommends potential projects for project selection	Provides support to the project selection process Assesses and recommends methods, tools, or models for use in project selection	Establishes a project selection process Consults with experts throughout the organization and externally as appropriate concerning project selection Establishes and issues a framework for a project charter Supports the preparation of the organization's strategic plan Identifies and appoints project managers	Authorizes projects to be undertaken by the organization Selects the optimum mix of projects in support of the organization's business strategy Ensures each project supports the ongoing work of the organization and the organization's business strategy Prepares the organization's strategic plan in terms of projects to pursue Issues project charters

Process/Position	Project Team Member	Associate Project Manager	Project Manager	PMO Staff Member	PMO Director	Vice President of Projects
Scope Planning	Uses state-of-the-art techniques to perform a product analysis Collects, analyzes, and documents project requirements in alignment with organizational strategy Identifies objectives linked to deliverables, requirements, assumptions, and constraints	Prepares benefit/cost analysis on project alternatives Supports the preparation of the project's scope management plan	Prepares and issues the project's scope statement Prepares and issues the project's scope management plan Ensures that quantitative objectives are established for the project success criteria Conducts planning meetings with stakeholders to collect and analyze requirements Ensures product requirements reflect agreed-upon customer needs	Identifies tools and techniques for use in the organization to support product analysis Identifies methodologies to use for benefit/cost analyses	Establishes requirements for the scope statement for each project Establishes requirements for the scope management plan	Evaluates perceived value and overall impact of the project on customers

Scope Definition	Provides support in the development of the WBS	Reviews historical data for use in scope definition Reviews existing WBS templates for use on the project Provides support in the development of the WBS Establishes a unique identifier for each item in the WBS Establishes and maintains the WBS dictionary	Issues the project's WBS	Develops WBS templates for use on projects throughout the organization Establishes standard coding structures for each project's WBS Establishes a format for a WBS dictionary for use on projects Provides support to inspections and reviews
Scope Verification	Conducts inspections of work products to determine whether results conform to requirements	Maintains product documentation Ensures scope verification is performed in parallel with quality control	Reviews work results and deliverables to ensure all were completed satisfactorily Obtains formal acceptance of project scope from stakeholders	

Process/Position	Project Team Member	Associate Project Manager	Project Manager	PMO Staff Member	PMO Director	Vice President of Projects
Scope Change Control	Analyzes scope change requests Prepares and submits change requests for decision as to approval, deferral, or disapproval	Integrates scope change control with other control processes Reviews performance reports for issues involving scope changes Identifies lessons learned Establishes a scope change control system for the project	Makes decisions on requested scope changes to the technical baseline Prevents unauthorized or incorrect changes from being included in the technical baseline Takes corrective action as required Revises and reissues baseline documents as required Identifies, analyzes, and reports lessons learned to the knowledge management system	Provides assistance in use of performance measurement techniques to help assess the magnitude of variances on projects Collects lessons learned in scope control for the knowledge management system	Establishes and analyzes project scope management metrics Analyzes lessons learned in scope control Uses the results of lessons learned in project scope management for improvements to the project management practice	
Activity Definition	Participates in the development of the activity list	Reviews historical data for use in defining activities Reviews existing templates for use in the activity definition process	Defines activities so project objectives can be met Issues the activity list	Develops activity list templates for use on projects		

Activity Sequencing	Identifies mandatory, external, discretionary dependencies	Identifies methods to use for activity sequencing Reviews existing network templates for use on the project	Issues the project's network diagram	Identifies methods to use for activity sequencing Develops network templates for use on projects Provides assistance in the use of conditional diagramming methods
Activity Duration Estimating	Develops durations for input to schedule development on specific activities Estimates work periods required to complete specific activities Considers information on identified risks in the estimating process	Reviews historical activity duration information from previous projects Uses computerized scheduling software during the estimating process	Estimates overall project duration Assesses resource requirements Identifies constraints and assumptions for activity duration estimating Consults with experts in estimating durations	Provides assistance in the use of estimating methodologies

Process/Position	Project Team Member	Associate Project Manager	Project Manager	PMO Staff Member	PMO Director	Vice President of Projects
Schedule Development	Determines lead and lag requirements between activities	Prepares and maintains project and resource calendars	Determines realistic start and finish dates	Provides support in the use of mathematical analysis techniques for schedule development	Provides information on the resources that will be available by assessing resource pool descriptions	
	Establishes and maintains resource calendars	Identifies and documents activity attributes	Identifies time constraints affecting the project	Provides support in the use of duration compression techniques	Establishes standard project management software for use in the organization	
		Uses mathematical analysis techniques for schedule development	Issues the project schedule	Provides support in the use of simulation techniques to calculate multiple project durations with different sets of activity assumptions	Establishes a standard coding structure for activities for use in the organization	
		Uses duration compression techniques based on specific project constraints and assumptions	Prepares and issues the project's schedule management plan	Provides support in resource leveling approaches	Reviews project schedules to identify dependencies across projects	
		Calculates multiple project durations with different sets of activity assumptions	Establishes the schedule baseline	Provides support in use of project management software	Establishes requirements for the schedule management plan	
		Uses resource leveling approaches				
		Uses project management software				

Schedule Control					
Identifies and analyzes schedule changes Prepares and submits change requests as necessary	Integrates schedule control with other control processes Reviews performance reports for issues on schedule performance Uses performance measurement techniques to assess the magnitude of schedule variations Uses project management software to track planned dates versus actual and to forecast the effects of schedule changes	Makes decisions on requested schedule changes to the schedule baseline Prevents unauthorized or incorrect changes from being included in the schedule baseline Measures and reports schedule performance to stakeholders Informs stakeholders of authorized changes and schedule revisions	Provides a coding structure for project activities Supports the preparation of the schedule management plan	Keeps abreast of developments in project management software to determine if changes in the organization's standard software packages are required Provides assistance in the use of performance measurement techniques for schedule control Collects lessons learned on projects in schedule control for the knowledge management system	Establishes and analyzes metrics for project time management Analyzes lessons learned in schedule control for improvements to the project management practice

Process/Position	Project Team Member	Associate Project Manager	Project Manager	PMO Staff Member	PMO Director	Vice President of Projects
		Conducts variance analysis / Establishes a schedule change control system for the project / Identifies lessons learned	Updates and issues revised schedules / Takes corrective action as a result of schedule changes / Identifies, analyzes, and reports lessons learned to the knowledge management system			
Resource Planning	Provides information on resource requirements for assigned work packages	Uses project management software for resource calendars	Identifies project deliverables and processes that will need resources / Determines when resources will be required and the specific quantities needed / Obtains people resources through staff acquisition or procurement	Uses project management software to help organize resource pools, define availability, and maintain information on resource rates / Forecasts resource requirements	Provides information about potential availability of resources	Establishes policies regarding staffing and the rental or purchase of supplies and equipment

Cost Estimating	Considers the extent to which the effect of risk is included in the cost estimates for each activity Estimates the cost of individual activities and work packages	Assigns the project cost estimates to the correct accounting category in the organization's chart of accounts Uses computerized tools to assist with cost estimating Supports the preparation of cost estimates Supports the preparation of the cost management plan	Prepares and issues the cost estimate for the project Identifies and considers costing alternatives, which may affect the project Prepares and issues the project's cost management plan	Supports use of life-cycle costing and value engineering techniques Provides information on resource rates for use in cost estimating Maintains commercially available data on cost estimating Provides support in the use of parametric models and in computerized tools to support cost estimating Analyzes information to determine specific financial impact to the project	Establishes a life-cycle costing system for the organization Predicts and analyzes prospective financial performance of the project's product Considers the cost of project decisions on the cost of using the project's product Establishes requirements for the cost management plan	Determines the pricing strategy for the project's product
Cost Budgeting	Allocates the overall cost estimate to individual activities Assigns costs to the time period when the cost will be incurred	Establishes the cost baseline for measuring project performance Establishes a spending plan or cash-flow forecast			Approves the project's budget Identifies and resolves budget discrepancies Establishes cost targets for projects	

Process/Position	Project Team Member	Associate Project Manager	Project Manager	PMO Staff Member	PMO Director	Vice President of Projects
Cost Control	Prepares and submits change requests for budget increases as necessary. Analyzes change requests submitted by others for cost implications on assigned work packages	Ensures that controllable and uncontrollable costs are estimated and budgeted separately to ensure rewards reflect performance. Reviews performance reports for issues on cost performance. Establishes a cost change control system for the project. Integrates cost control with other control processes. Uses performance measurement techniques to help assess the magnitude of cost variations. Establishes control account plans. Identifies lessons learned	Makes decisions on requested changes to the cost baseline. Monitors cost performance to detect and analyze variances from the plan. Prevents unauthorized or incorrect changes from being included in the cost baseline. Informs stakeholders of authorized changes and revised cost estimates. Updates and issues revised cost estimates. Acts to bring expected costs within acceptable limits	Provides support in the use of performance measurement techniques for cost control. Provides support in the use of computerized tools for project cost management. Collects lessons learned on projects in cost control for the knowledge management system	Establishes and analyzes metrics for project cost management. Analyzes lessons learned in schedule control. Analyzes lessons learned for improvements to the project management practice	

Quality Planning							
Reviews standards and regulations for quality implications Reviews the product description for issues affecting quality planning Designs experiments to identify technical factors that might influence specific variables in terms of the product of the project	Prepares benefit/cost analysis as part of quality planning Reviews existing checklists for applicability to the project Supports the preparation of the project's quality management plan	Rebaselines the project when required according to cost variances Forecasts estimates of a completion Identifies, analyzes, and reports lessons learned to the knowledge management system	Reviews the organization's quality policy to determine whether changes are required to support the individual project Identifies which quality standards are relevant to the project and determines how to satisfy them Prepares and issues the project's quality management plan	Provides support in the use of quality planning techniques Designs experiments to identify factors in project management that might influence specific variables	Provides standard definitions for quality and quality management on projects Establishes requirements for the quality management plan Participates in benchmarking forums external to the organization Establishes a system for internal benchmarking for projects	Establishes the organization's quality policy for projects Ensures the quality management standards are compatible with international standards Authorizes investments in product quality improvement

Process/Position	Project Team Member	Associate Project Manager	Project Manager	PMO Staff Member	PMO Director	Vice President of Projects
	Uses flowcharting to show how elements of the project relate		Establishes the project's project quality system		Establishes checklists for quality planning activities	
Quality Assurance	Prepares and submits change requests for quality improvement activities	Reviews quality control measurements Provides support to quality audits	Implements quality improvement actions to increase the effectiveness and efficiency of the product Establishes responsibility for quality assurance on the project Requests that quality audits be conducted	Participates in quality and project audits	Conducts quality and project audits Implements quality improvement actions in the project management practice Collects external data on best practices, new ideas, barriers, and risks	
Quality Control	Conducts inspections of work results and the final product of the project to ensure results conform to requirements	Monitors specific project results to determine if they comply with quality standards Uses quality control techniques to help analyze problems Conducts trend analysis	Establishes responsibility for quality control on the project Determines required rework as a result of non-acceptance decisions	Provides support in the use of quality control techniques Collects lessons learned on projects in quality control for the knowledge management system	Establishes and analyzes project quality metrics Assesses process adjustments in terms of the project management practice	

	Completes checklists used so they are part of the project's records Integrates quality control with other control processes Ensures quality control is performed in parallel with scope verification Identifies lessons learned	Takes corrective or preventive action as a result of quality control measurements Identifies, analyzes, and reports lessons learned to the knowledge management system		
Organizational Planning	Reviews available templates for organization planning for use on the project Supports the preparation of the Responsibility Assignment Matrix Supports the preparation of the Organizational Breakdown Structure Supports the preparation of the staffing management plan	Assigns project roles and responsibilities Establishes project reporting relationships Assesses project interfaces Determines staffing requirements in terms of the kinds of competencies required from what kinds of individuals or groups and in what time periods	Establishes templates for use in organizational planning	Prepares job descriptions for project management positions Assesses the impact of various organizational alternatives Establishes requirements for the staffing management plan	Establishes project organizational structures

Process/Position	Project Team Member	Associate Project Manager	Project Manager	PMO Staff Member	PMO Director	Vice President of Projects
			Prepares and issues the Organizational Breakdown Structure Prepares and issues the Resource Assignment Matrix Conducts a stakeholder analysis Prepares and issues the staffing management plan Determines training requirements for project team members			
Staff Acquisition		Remains cognizant of the organization's human resource management administrative requirements Prepares a project team directory	Obtains needed human resources for work on the project Assesses characteristics of potentially available staff Negotiates staff assignments		Supports the project manager as required in staff negotiations	Establishes recruitment practices for project management Establishes incentives for staff assignments in project management

Team Development						
Prepares an individual development plan Assesses performance on the project against the expectations of those outside the project Provides input to performance appraisals of team members as requested	Establishes a "war-" room or a "team" room Prepares an individual development plan Identifies lessons learned	Prepares an individual development plan Ensures people involved with the project are used effectively Resolves conflicts on the project team Holds a kick-off meeting Conducts team-building activities Prepares performance appraisals Identifies team performance improvements Identifies, analyzes, and reports lessons learned to the knowledge management system	Prepares an individual development plan Provides mentoring support Provides facilitation services for team development Collects lessons learned	Establishes mentoring relationships Establishes a project reward and recognition system Establishes a project management training program Establishes a project management career path Assesses improvements in individual or team competencies Conducts performance appraisals Analyzes lessons learned for improvements to the project management practice	Ensures that the organization's reward and recognition system supports the project-based reward and recognition systems Establishes a budget for project management training including direct and indirect costs

Process/Position	Project Team Member	Associate Project Manager	Project Manager	PMO Staff Member	PMO Director	Vice President of Projects
Communications Planning	Determines project communication requirements Conducts a stakeholder analysis of information needs	Makes information available to project stakeholders Establishes technologies for project information transfer Establishes a distribution structure for project information Establishes a method to gather and store project information Establishes a schedule to show when each type of communication will be produced Supports the preparation of the project's communications management plan	Prepares and issues the project's communications management plan Determines the information and communications needs of project stakeholders Identifies constraints and assumptions affecting communication planning	Identifies communication technologies or methods to use to transfer information	Sets standards for communication technology methods to use to transfer information for projects Establishes requirements for the communications management plan	

Information Distribution		Establishes an information retrieval system for the project / Prepares a project newsletter / Distributes project information / Maintains project records	Prepares formal project reports / Conducts project presentations		Attends project presentations
Performance Reporting	Prepares change requests as a result of analysis of project performance as necessary	Uses earned value analysis / Performs trend analysis / Performs variance analysis	Prepares status reports / Prepares progress reports / Predicts future project status and progress / Conducts performance reviews	Provides support in the use of earned value analysis	Conducts project performance reviews / Establishes and analyzes project metrics
Administrative Closure	Completes project documentation / Supports the preparation of a project closeout plan	Prepares an indexed set of project records for archiving / Documents lessons learned / Supports the preparation of a project closeout plan	Reviews project documentation to ensure it is complete / Prepares and issues a project closeout plan / Analyzes project success, effectiveness, and lessons learned	Collects lessons learned on projects for the knowledge management system	Analyzes lessons learned for improvements to the project management practice / Establishes requirements for the project closeout plan

Process/Position	Project Team Member	Associate Project Manager	Project Manager	PMO Staff Member	PMO Director	Vice President of Projects
			Identifies and reports lessons learned to the knowledge management system. Confirms that the project has met all customer requirements. Receives formal acceptance from the customer that the project is complete			
Risk Management Planning	Supports the preparation of the project's risk management plan	Reviews organizational policies regarding risk. Supports the preparation of the project's risk management plan	Assesses stakeholder tolerances for risk. Conducts meetings with the team and other stakeholders to prepare the risk management plan. Prepares and issues the project risk management plan	Prepares a template for the project's risk management plan	Establishes requirements for the risk management plan	Establishes a culture that supports open communication on risks. Establishes organizational risk management policies

Risk Identification	Uses state-of-the-art information-gathering techniques to identify risks Conducts interviews to identify risks	Reviews historical data from previous projects concerning risks encountered Reviews risk categories established for use in risk identification	Establishes roles and responsibilities for each action in the risk management plan Establishes a budget for risk management on the project Determines how often the risk management process will be performed or the project Establishes threshold criteria for risks to be acted upon Performs a structured review of plans, constraints, and assumptions to identify risks Prepares a list of identified risks Establishes triggers for potential risks	Provides facilitation support for the use of Delphi Analysis in risk identification Develops checklists for risk identification Provides support in the use of risk identification techniques	Analyzes data on project risks and their characteristics for use in the knowledge management system

Process/Position	Project Team Member	Associate Project Manager	Project Manager	PMO Staff Member	PMO Director	Vice President of Projects
Qualitative Risk Analysis	Supports probability and risk impact assessment analyses	Uses qualitative analysis methods and tools to analyze risk Evaluates risk probability and risk consequences Prepares a probability/impact risk rating matrix Tests and analyzes project assumptions Evaluates the degree to which data about risks are useful for risk management	Assesses the impact and likelihood of identified risks Assesses trends based on the results of the qualitative analysis of risks Prepares an overall risk ranking for the project Prepares a list of prioritized risks Prepares a list of risks for additional analysis and management	Identifies techniques for qualitative risk analysis Provides support in the use of qualitative analysis methods and tools to identify risks	Establishes categories for risks that may affect projects based on common sources of risk for the industry and application area Establishes information of the probability of occurrence of risk events and their consequences for projects of a common or recurrent type	

Quantitative Risk Analysis	Conducts interviews to quantify the probability and consequences of risks on project objectives	Quantifies the relative contribution of each risk to the project Uses tools and techniques for quantitative risk analysis	Identifies realistic and achievable cost, schedule, or scope targets Assesses trends based on the results of the quantitative analysis of risks Consults experts as part of the quantitative analysis process Prepares a prioritized list of quantified risks	Identifies techniques for quantitative risk analysis Provides support in the use of quantitative risk analysis techniques	Establishes thresholds of the level of risk acceptable to the organization
Risk Response Planning	Recommends risk response strategies based on analyses conducted Identifies residual and secondary risks	Recommends risk response strategies for the key risks that may affect the project Supports the preparation of the risk response plan	Selects appropriate risk responses from possible options Identifies people to act as owners of risk responses Determines contingency allowances for accepted risks Prepares and issues risk response plans		Identifies common risk causes that affect the organization's projects Establishes requirements for risk response plans

Process/Position	Project Team Member	Associate Project Manager	Project Manager	PMO Staff Member	PMO Director	Vice President of Projects
Risk Monitoring and Control	Prepares and submits change requests as a result of implementation of contingency plans or workarounds as necessary	Establishes a risk database or repository. Identifies lessons learned	Prepares contingency and fallback plans. Enters into contractual agreements for specific risks. Conducts project risk reviews. Assesses results of risk responses for lessons learned. Uses workarounds for unidentified or accepted risks. Identifies, analyzes, and reports lessons learned to the knowledge management system	Conducts project risk audits. Updates risk identification checklists. Collects lessons learned on projects in risk monitoring and control for the knowledge management system	Incorporates information on risk responses into the knowledge management system and analyzes results for improvements to the project management practice	
Procurement Planning	Provides support to the preparation of the statement(s) of work	Supports the preparation of the procurement management plan	Performs make-or-buy analyses. Identifies procurement planning constraints and assumptions			Establishes make-or-buy policies

Solicitation Planning	Supports the preparation of procurement documents Prepares evaluation criteria to rate or score proposals	Ensures evaluation criteria are complete and will meet the needs of the upcoming procurements	Consults with procurement planning experts Prepares and issues the procurement management plan	Establishes roles and responsibilities for project teams and project managers and members of the organization's procurement department Establishes requirements for the procurement management plan
Solicitation			Arranges for the preparation of independent estimates Supports the procurement department during bidder conferences	Provides information based on lessons learned to the procurement department for use with qualified seller lists

Process/Position	Project Team Member	Associate Project Manager	Project Manager	PMO Staff Member	PMO Director	Vice President of Projects
Source Selection	Supports the proposal evaluation process Provides input into the establishment of weighting and screening systems	Assists in evaluation of proposals	Evaluates proposals Rank orders proposals to establish a negotiation sequence			
Contract Administration	Monitors seller performance Prepares and submits change requests for contract modifications as necessary Reviews seller invoices	Integrates the contract change control system with the other project control systems	Coordinates the management of multiple providers Coordinates procurements with other aspects of the project			
Contract Closeout		Ensures contractual documentation is complete Identifies lessons learned	Ensures seller's work was completed satisfactorily Identifies, analyzes and reports lessons learned to the knowledge management system	Collects lessons learned on projects in project procurement management for the knowledge management system	Analyzes lessons learned for improvements to the project management practice	

APPENDIX 4C
KNOWLEDGE
AND COMPETENCY
REQUIREMENTS
BY PROJECT POSITION

Process/Position	Project Team Member	Associate Project Manager	Project Manager	PMO Staff Member	Director, PMO	Vice President of Projects
Project Plan Development	Planning processes Project life cycle Contents of a project plan	Project management software Existing project documents Documentation management Planning processes Project life cycle Contents of a project plan	Planning methodologies Contents of a project plan Planning processes Project management methodology contents Assumption identification techniques Constraint identification techniques Communications techniques Tactical planning	Planning processes Contents of a project plan Project life cycle Project management software Project management methodology contents	Project management methodologies and tools Planning methodologies Internal project environments Organizational policies Project management strategies Establishing metrics Social-economic-environmental influences	Planning strategies External project environment Policy development Strategic planning Social-economic-environmental sustainability
Project Plan Execution	Executing processes Product-specific/technical requirements Phase-end requirements Tracking performance against a plan	Executing processes Project management software Earned value analysis Tracking performance against a plan	Executing processes Problem solving Workload balancing techniques Motivational techniques Communications techniques	Executing processes Project management software Methods analysis	Organizational policies Problem solving Internationalization Meeting management techniques	Establishing direction Internationalization Policy analysis Program evaluation Influencing the organization

Integrated Change Control	Methods to prepare and analyze change requests	Preparing meeting agendas and taking minutes of meetings	Management/leadership principles and techniques Meeting management techniques	Decision-making processes		
	Controlling processes Tracking and monitoring techniques Data collection techniques Methods to prepare and analyze change requests Reporting changes	Controlling processes Earned value management techniques Configuration management software Documentation management Tracking and monitoring Project management software Integration methodologies	Controlling processes Gathering, assessing, and integrating information Change management techniques Lessons learned identification	Controlling processes Earned value management techniques Configuration management software Knowledge management approaches	Gathering, assessing, and integrating information Knowledge management	Decision-making processes
Initiation	Initiating process Requirements gathering and analysis techniques Available requirements Available specifications	Initiating process Requirements tools and methodologies	Initiating process Communications techniques Requirements analysis methods Stakeholder identification techniques	Initiating process Benefit-measurement methods Constrained-optimization methods	Organizational project management policies and procedures Project requirements and objectives	Decision-making processes Corporate culture Functional business areas Strategic planning Economic value added

Process/Position	Project Team Member	Associate Project Manager	Project Manager	PMO Staff Member	Director, PMO	Vice President of Projects
Scope Planning	Product analysis techniques (systems engineering, value engineering, value analysis, function analysis, quality function deployment (QFD))	Benefit/cost analysis techniques	Methods to establish quantifiable criteria; Planning methodologies; Meeting management techniques; Stakeholder expectations; New product development methodologies	Product analysis techniques (systems engineering, value engineering, value analysis, function analysis, QFD); Benefit/cost analysis techniques	Resource skills and categories; Decision-making processes; Resource selection criteria and techniques; Level of authority; Assumption identification techniques; Constraint identification techniques; Planning methodologies; Establishing metrics	Stakeholder expectations; Organizational influences; Strategic planning; Economic value added

Scope Definition	Existing project documents Purpose and uses of a WBS	Existing project documents Purpose and uses of a WBS Documentation management	WBS development and decomposition techniques Purpose and uses of a WBS	WBS decomposition techniques Purpose and uses of a WBS	Knowledge management (WBS templates)
Scope Verification	Inspection techniques	Inspection techniques Documentation management	Acceptance processes Authorization procedures	Inspection techniques	Acceptance processes Approving authorities
Scope Change Control	Tracking and monitoring techniques Data collection techniques Methods to prepare and analyze change requests Reporting changes	Performance measurement techniques Integration methodologies	Scope and change management techniques Lessons learned identification	Performance measurement techniques	Knowledge management
Activity Definition	Existing project documents Purpose of the activity list	Existing project documents Purpose of the activity list PDM and ADM techniques	Decomposition techniques Purpose of the activity list	Existing project documents Purpose of the activity list PDM, ADM, and conditional diagramming techniques	Knowledge management (activity list templates)
Activity Sequencing	Product characteristics Types of dependencies		Integrating and sequencing activities and tasks Assumption identification techniques		Knowledge management (network templates)

Process/Position	Project Team Member	Associate Project Manager	Project Manager	PMO Staff Member	Director, PMO	Vice President of Projects
Activity Duration Estimating	Existing project documents Risk identification methods Bottom-up estimating approach	Computerized estimating tools and techniques	Constraint identification techniques Estimating techniques Assumption identification techniques Constraint identification techniques Resource identification techniques	Computerized estimating tools and techniques		
Schedule Development	Project activity characteristics Project and resource calendars	Resource leveling techniques CPM and PERT Crashing and fast tracking Project management software	Planning methodologies Presentation techniques (Gantt, milestone, network) Constraint identification techniques	Resource leveling techniques CPM, PERT, GERT Crashing and fast tracking Critical chain (Monte Carlo) Simulation Project management software	Establishing metrics	
Schedule Control	Tracking and monitoring techniques	Performance measurement techniques	Change management techniques	Earned value management techniques	Knowledge management	

	Data collection techniques Methods to prepare and analyze change requests Reporting changes	Earned value management techniques Project management software Variance analysis techniques Integration methodologies	Lessons learned identification Performance measurement techniques	Project management software		
Resource Planning	Existing project documents Identifying resource requirements	Project management software	Resource estimating techniques Negotiation techniques	Project management software	Establishing metrics Knowledge management Organizational policies	Policy analysis
Cost Estimating	Product requirements Bottom-up cost estimating approach Risk identification techniques	Computerized estimating tools and techniques	Planning methodologies Costing alternatives Estimating methodologies	ROI, payback analysis, discounted cash flow analysis Estimating publications Computerized estimating tools and techniques Parametric modeling	Life-cycle costing Value engineering Costing alternatives	Marketing analysis
Cost Budgeting	Tracking and monitoring	Budgeting controllable and uncontrollable costs Cost allocation	Budget management techniques Cost allocation	Tracking and monitoring	Organizational policies	

Process/Position	Project Team Member	Associate Project Manager	Project Manager	PMO Staff Member	Director, PMO	Vice President of Projects
Cost Control	Tracking and monitoring techniques Data collection techniques Methods to prepare and analyze change requests Reporting changes	Performance measurement techniques Earned value management techniques Project management software Integration methodologies	Change management techniques Forecasting Lessons learned identification Performance measurement techniques Stakeholder management	Earned value management techniques Project management software	Knowledge management	
Quality Planning	Statistics QFD Product requirements Flowcharting Standards and regulations	Statistics Standards and regulations Benefit/cost analysis	Planning methodologies Assessing applicable standards	Statistics QFD Designing experiments	Establishing metrics Benchmarking	Industry standards Policy development
Quality Assurance	Tracking and monitoring Methods to prepare and analyze change requests	Industry product and service standards Quality control measures	Quality assurance standards and techniques Lessons learned identification	Industry product and service standards Auditing practices and procedures Interviewing techniques	Quality assurance standards and techniques Knowledge management	Policy analysis and evaluation

Element						
Quality Control	Statistics; Data collection techniques; Inspections; Flowcharting; Methods to prepare and analyze change requests	Control limits; Statistical sampling; Trend analysis; Tracking and monitoring	Adjusting processes; Acceptance decisions	Control limits; Statistical sampling; Trend analysis	Organization-specific checklists and procedures for managing, and benefiting from, historical data; Adjusting processes	
Organizational Planning	Purpose of the responsibility assignment matrix; Purpose of the organizational breakdown structure	Resource estimating techniques; Workload balancing techniques; Organizational policies and procedures; Planning methodologies; Project interfaces; Constraint identification techniques; Stakeholder analysis techniques			Organizational policies and procedures; Establishing metrics; Project interfaces; Competency analysis; Knowledge management (organizational templates)	Organizational theory; Organizational behavior

Process/Position	Project Team Member	Associate Project Manager	Project Manager	PMO Staff Member	Director, PMO	Vice President of Projects
Staff Acquisition		Documentation management	Negotiation techniques Resource sources and availability Human resource management policies		Human resource management policies Competency analysis	Human resource management policies
Team Development	Self-assessment Professional responsibility Tracking and monitoring	Self-assessment Professional responsibility Documentation management	Professional responsibility Facilitation techniques Team-building methods and techniques Motivational techniques Conflict resolution techniques Recognition options Stress management Self-assessment Appreciation of cultural differences Meeting management	Professional responsibility Facilitation techniques Self-assessment	Professional responsibility Self-assessment Stress management Appreciation of cultural differences Organizational policy analysis (reward and recognition) Knowledge management (performance improvement)	Policy development (reward and recognition) Professional responsibility Aligning people

Communications Planning	Requirements analysis methodologies Stakeholder analysis	Technology analysis Information transfer approaches	Communications management concepts Planning methodologies Constraint identification techniques Stakeholder analysis	Technology analysis	Establishing metrics
Information Distribution	Report preparation	Retrieval systems Distribution methodologies Documentation management	Communications management tools and techniques Stakeholder management Reporting techniques Presentation techniques	Distribution methodologies	
Performance Reporting	Data collection techniques Methods to prepare and analyze change requests	Performance measurement techniques Reporting (production and requirements) Resource utilization Earned value management techniques	Presentation techniques Reporting techniques Performance measurement techniques	Earned value management techniques Performance measurement techniques	Review standards and frequency Program evaluation methodologies

Process/Position	Project Team Member	Associate Project Manager	Project Manager	PMO Staff Member	Director, PMO	Vice President of Projects
Administrative Closure	Closing processes Existing project documents	Trend analysis Documentation management Closing processes Existing project documents Archiving methodologies	Closing processes Customer requirements Resource re-deployment planning Lessons learned identification	Closing processes Archiving methodologies	Acceptance processes Knowledge management Program evaluation methodologies	
Risk Management Planning			Assumption identification methods Constraint identification methods Risk management concepts Planning methodologies Role and responsibility definition Meeting management		Establishing metrics Knowledge management (template for planning)	Corporate culture Policy development Risk tolerance analysis

Risk Identification	Interviewing techniques Existing project documents Document analysis techniques Brainstorming	Existing project documents Facilitation techniques Diagramming techniques	Assumptions analysis Establishing warning indications Document analysis techniques	Facilitation techniques Diagramming techniques	Knowledge management (risk categories)
Qualitative Risk Analysis		Probability/impact analysis Data reliability analysis	Assumption identification techniques Assumptions testing methodologies Trend analysis Prioritization approaches	Data precision analysis Probability/impact analysis	Trend analysis
Quantitative Risk Analysis	Interviewing techniques	Sensitivity analysis Decision tree analysis Interviewing techniques	Trend analysis Prioritization approaches	Monte Carlo simulation Decision tree analysis Sensitivity analysis	Trend analysis
Risk Response Planning	Risk identification techniques Risk analysis techniques		Workload management Planning methodologies Contractual approaches		Knowledge management (risk causes)

Process/Position	Project Team Member	Associate Project Manager	Project Manager	PMO Staff Member	Director, PMO	Vice President of Projects
Risk Monitoring and Control	Tracking and monitoring Methods to prepare and analyze change requests	Earned value analysis Data management	Change management techniques Lessons learned identification Performance reviews	Auditing techniques Interviewing techniques Earned value analysis	Trend analysis Review methodologies	
Procurement Planning	Product analysis Procurement document requirements	Make-or-buy analysis techniques	Procurement guidelines and regulations Planning methodologies Assumption identification techniques Constraint identification techniques Types of contracts Make-or-buy analysis techniques	Marketing research and analysis	Establishing metrics	
Solicitation Planning	Existing project documents Procurement document requirements	Existing project documents	Types of contracts Criteria analysis Estimating approaches		Types of contracts	

Solicitation				
Source Selection	Evaluation techniques		Meeting management techniques; Evaluation methodologies; Negotiation techniques	
Contract Administration	Tracking and monitoring; Methods to prepare and analyze change requests	Payment analysis techniques; Change management techniques	Administration of contracts; Legal requirements	Administration of contracts; Legal requirements
Contract Closeout	Document review		Closing procedures; Acceptance procedures; Lessons learned identification	Knowledge management

5

MATURITY MODELS

5.1 OVERVIEW

How do you know if your projects are truly contributing to the success and growth of your organization? An organization with a progressive standard to foster project management improvement responds to this challenge by establishing a metrics program, conducting a project management maturity assessment, and using a project management maturity model.

It has long been recognized that sound measurement practices are integral to basic project management activities such as project planning, project monitoring, and project control. As organizations mature in terms of project management and as more organizations follow a managing by projects approach, management that is objective and performance based relies heavily on measurement practices. Metrics need to be integrated into project life-cycle processes to support decision making, project selection, and portfolio management and to guide product and process improvement. Metrics are ever present throughout project management. Metrics can serve as indicators of organizational project management maturity. Metrics help organizations understand capabilities so that achievable plans for producing and delivering products and services can be developed. Metrics enable people to identify important events and trends. Metrics can help project professionals separate problems from opportunities. Thus, metrics can help provide better control of costs and schedules, reduce risks, improve quality, and ensure that objectives can be achieved (O'Hara and Levin, 2000).

Unfortunately, organizations often use metrics incorrectly. They may not collect any metrics at all, or they may collect a lot of metrics but have no valuable use of the data that are collected. They may collect data but use only a small part of the information that can be gleaned from the data. Some metrics are only collected to fulfill a corporate requirement such as to report on information at certain dates. At the other end of the spectrum, in some organizations, measurement is an end unto itself. One danger is that there are potentially so many things to measure that one can become overwhelmed by opportunities. It is important to plan a metrics program by identifying project and process management issues, by selecting and defining the corresponding metrics, and by integrating them into existing processes.

Metrics, as used here, are small measurable quantities that have a predictive or measurement capability; they can offer a glimpse of the status of an item relative to expectations. A good metric is one that contributes to the right decisions in a timely way, and is based on fact rather than feeling (Augustine and Schroeder, 1999). Metrics can identify important events and trends in the organization and can help guide the organization toward informed decisions. They can serve as the basis for clear, objective communication with project stakeholders. Metrics are a basic tool used to monitor and aid in determining the health of any set of processes. They can be used to measure the status of activities, take a process view, and gauge the contribution of project management to the organization (Dymond, 1995). Metrics can also be used to show where an organization stands in terms of project management maturity.

In the same fashion that project evaluation models measure the sophistication of the project team in carrying out the missions of a single project, an organizational project management maturity model measures the ability of the collective organizational project management staff to deliver projects meeting specifications, on time, and within budget. Therefore, although maturity models collect data on a project-by-project basis, they are organizational tools rather than project-specific tools. The models expand the scope from the single project to the enterprise since the overall success of projects and project management is highly dependent on how well the organizational environment supports and enables project managers to achieve success in their projects. Primarily, a project management maturity model describes the key elements of a fully effective project management environment. These elements are then used for the purposes of benchmarking and evaluation. Considering the presence or absence of these elements, one can arrive at a ranking of levels one to five for the maturity of the project management processes of an organization.

Maturity, according to the *Random House Dictionary*, is defined as full development or a perfected condition. It also connotes understanding or visibility as to why success occurs, and as to ways to prevent common problems. In terms of project management, this relates to capabilities that can produce repeatable success in project management (Schlichter, 1999). Kerzner further notes (2000, p. 32) that "all organizations go through a maturity process, and that this maturity process must precede excellence.

The learning curve for maturity is measured in years." He states (2001) that companies that mature in project management, and reach some degree of excellence, achieve and exploit a sustained competitive advantage.

The early models developed for assessing organizational project management maturity used a 1-to-5 scale. There is nothing inherently compelling about this scale, and the logic is more historical than technical. Notwithstanding any shortcomings, most models fortuitously use the same scale. Thus, organizational ratings can be compared across industries and even between models.

If there are formalized and quantitative procedures in arriving at an organization's maturity ranking, then such a carefully determined ranking will provide a clearly defined indicator of an organization's capabilities in managing projects. The maturity ranking is affected by project objectives, project management practices, organizational infrastructure, organizational objectives, and organizational commitment. Maturity ranking is further influenced by personnel capability, clarity and specificity of procedures, and organizational performance in assignment of ample resources to projects. Tracking the organizational maturity status on a regular basis will serve as an indicator of how effectively an organization is meeting its goals in managing projects and in meeting business objectives.

A maturity model can be used to determine the existence of realistic and effective project management policies and procedures. A serious distinction should be made between having procedures on the shelves in every office without ever using them and using the existing procedures on a regular basis. Further, the methodologies associated with a maturity model can be used to assess the effectiveness of the prevailing project management policies and procedures, which in turn will signal how often and how regularly the project personnel follow the established procedures. The established ranking scale of a maturity model will provide plateaus for the purposes of continuous improvement of project management capabilities. The plateau level indicators of the model highlight key elements of a specific facet of project management in the organization in order to identify key practices that need improvement to elevate the organization's ranking in that specific facet of project management. An added advantage of evaluating organizational capabilities using a standardized scale through a maturity model is that one can calculate indicators for industry-wide comparisons. That would provide a point of pride if the organization ranks favorably, and the motivation to improve if the organization ranks not so favorably.

Higher maturity levels signify more effective project procedures, higher-quality deliverables, lower project costs, higher project team morale, a desirable balance between cost–schedule–quality, and ultimately improved profits for the organization. The more mature organization is the one that can manage processes. In such an organization, there is an objective, quantitative basis for judging quality and analyzing problems. As such, expected results for cost, schedule, functionality, and quality are achieved. Further, roles and responsibilities are clearly defined, and customer satisfaction is expected, as the norm.

By contrast, lower maturity levels are normally consistent with organizational environments that encourage fixing problems in the field instead of doing it right the first time. Therefore, it is entirely possible that project personnel might repeat the same errors in multiple projects or even in the same project. A low ranking could also be a symptom of an organization that has unnecessary or redundant procedures, which in turn are usually concurrent with an organization having a history of misdirected improvement efforts. In an immature organization, there is no objective basis to judge product quality since processes are improvised, since activities to enhance quality are often curtailed or eliminated, and since there is no objective basis to judge or process problems. When hard deadlines are imposed, functionality and quality are often compromised to meet the schedule. In these organizations, people who are project managers primarily are similar to fire fighters, acting in a reactionary basis (Figure 5.1).

Benefits of using a project management maturity model include the ability to assess an organization's current project management capabilities and the ability to identify organizational strengths and weaknesses in project management. Further, the observations made with the use of a maturity model will provide the impetus to establish uniform project management practices within the organization, to provide capabilities for benefiting from one project's experience into the next project, and to formulate continuous improvement methodologies for project management procedures. The benefits of adopting and using evaluation models extend into the details of project performance by fostering improved project performance in the areas of cost, schedule, scope, and quality. The results of evaluation models further establish a baseline for improve-

■ Immature organization	■ Mature organization
■ Processes improvised	■ Organization-wide ability to manage processes
■ Reactionary	
■ People are fire fighters	■ Roles and responsibilities are defined and clear
■ Schedules and budgets exceeded	
■ Quality is difficult to predict	■ Customer satisfaction
	■ High-quality projects

Figure 5.1   Immature vs. Mature Organizations

ment objectives if the organization chooses to become project oriented with predictable project success rates. It is an important point that the focus of use of a maturity model is not to provide a quick fix for projects in trouble. The focus of an assessment is to provide the foundation for improvements and guidance for advancement.

5.2 MATURITY LEVELS

Figures 5.2 and 5.3 describe the five maturity levels. As indicated previously, most models use the same scale, patterned after that of the Software Engineering Institute in its Capability Maturity Model for Software, although the descriptions of the plateaus are worded somewhat differently. Maturity models methodically evaluate an organization's capabilities in managing the following project facets: scope, quality, cost, schedule, procurement, reporting, integration, risk, communication, team morale, vendor relations, and client relations. The levels of maturity define specific goals or objectives that are to be achieved. The goals or objectives at each maturity level are usually presented as results statements. These results statements describe observable milestones to verify whether or not an organization has effectively implemented certain processes. They describe key activities to be performed. As a progressive standard, the models state that reaching a higher level means reaching a higher level of maturity.

5	Optimizing, Adaptive
4	Comprehensive, Managed
3	Integrated, Organized, Defined
2	Consistent, Abbreviated, Repeatable
1	Ad hoc, Initial

Figure 5.2   Maturity Levels

5	Organizational Use of Quantitative Data to Conduct Continuous Improvement
4	Organization Commits to a PM Culture and Captures Quantified Performance Data
3	Organization Implements PM Processes and Gives Recognition to Successful PM Processes
2	Localized Implementation of Formalized PM Processes
1	Inconsistent Procedures and No Formal Guidelines

Figure 5.3   Maturity Level Descriptions

5.2.1 Level One

Level one is characterized as ad hoc or basic. Organizations at this level do not have formal project management procedures, and thus experience infrequent project performance predictability. Project management is performed inconsistently across the organization. It is highly probable that projects of these organizations experience cost overruns, schedule delays, and defective deliverables. Proper execution and on-time delivery are rare occurrences and are normally effected through heroics by the project team. Project management training is not provided. Isolated success stories are results of competent people, individual effort, and unusual sacrifices.

Rework is expected on projects because quality is imparted to the deliverable as a result of inspections rather than through plans. Inspections and audits are conducted primarily at the request of customers. Status reports and progress reports are prepared, and project reviews are held, only in response to customer requests. Many projects are not formally closed out, and therefore files are not archived and maintained in a fashion that promotes sharing of lessons learned, even if those lessons could be identified.

5.2.2 Level Two

Level two is described as consistent or repeatable. The emphasis is to introduce project management tools and techniques and have them accepted at the project level in the organization. If an organization is ranked at level two, then there are indications that a project management methodology has been adopted by the organization, and that project management roles and responsibilities are defined. Project plans are prepared according to established procedures, and probably there is a project management office. The PMO provides templates and forms to assist in the planning process. The PMO establishes a procedure for project planning, including lists of the desired contents of a project plan. The PMO also establishes some project management procedures to track cost schedule and performance. Proper and timely project management training is provided to the project team. Training topics include the generic project management competencies, but also instruction on the proper execution of the organization's project management procedures.

Level-two projects focus on disciplined formalized project management on all projects. Project management procedures result in visible effectiveness in managing cost, schedule, scope and quality. Project charters are prepared, a WBS is formulated and used, a project schedule is prepared and issued, and a schedule baseline is established for project control. In addition, resource planning is conducted, cost estimates are prepared, and a cost baseline is established for project control. Project problems are recognized quickly and corrected expeditiously. Quality audits and inspections are planned and conducted. Project roles and responsibilities are established, and team-building activities are conducted throughout the project life cycle. Project risks are identified, analyzed, and reviewed methodically, and response strategies are developed for the major risks. Procurement planning is conducted.

However, it is entirely possible that, in organizations at level two, underlying disciplines are not well understood or consistently followed. Therefore, project success still is largely unpredictable, and cost and schedule problems are the norm. But, there is a tendency to collect data and to evaluate the effectiveness of the plans that are in place and to assess project performance. Status reports are prepared, and project review meetings are held. Supplier and subcontractor performance is monitored and reviewed.

5.2.3 Level Three

Level three is described as integrated or structured. If an organization is ranked at level three, project management methodologies are integrated with other organizational procedures. As such, there is organizational commitment, focus, and support for compliance with processes and procedures. A level-three ranked organization has a centralized project management entity, the PMO, that facilitates functional units' understanding of basic project management practices; well-defined performance management policies; and a clear path for improvement of those policies and procedures. In these organizations, projects use software tools to manage multiple projects and to link resource usage between projects. Project management processes are documented, standardized, and integrated. Proper project management tools and techniques are adopted and used throughout the organization. Problems are methodically anticipated and efficiently prevented so their impacts are minimized. Information is collected, shared, and used across projects. Project teams work together in predefined structures, and training is planned and provided according to roles and responsibilities of project personnel.

The organization demonstrates its commitment to project management by establishing a PMO with specific responsibility for development and deployment of a standard project management methodology. The project management methodology includes an integrated change control system and standard templates for use in project planning, monitoring, and control. At the time that a project is initiated, the implementation methodology is reviewed to determine, given the nature of the project, whether a scaled version of the standard procedures is more appropriate. The PMO collects historical information and makes the information available throughout the organization for use in development of project plans. Life-cycle cost analysis is conducted regularly. The PMO routinely conducts reviews of activities in terms of scope, cost, schedule, quality, human resources, communications, and procurement. Another function of the PMO is to collect metrics to assess project performance on a project-by-project basis and across the organization and to analyze the trends. The PMO continually refines project checklists so that they are increasingly more effective. The PMO documents causes of variances for lessons learned, and establishes a repository for project documentation. Working in partnership with the Procurement Department, the PMO establishes a lessons-learned database as procurement information is archived for future use.

The PMO also develops, implements, and maintains a standard project management information system (PMIS). The PMIS supports the measurement of scope, schedule, cost, resources, quality, communications, and changes in project environment. It also supports risk identification and reporting. The PMO provides training in the use of the PMIS, because the same PMIS is used consistently on all projects. There are standard features in the PMIS to be used by all projects and the ability for customization to meet the unique needs of each project.

Further, the PMO is responsible for project management training by establishing a standard curriculum throughout the organization. Typically, the PMO funds the indirect and direct costs of training activities, so these costs are not part of a specific project's budget.

5.2.4 Level Four

Level four is described as comprehensive or integrated. In these organizations, there is organizational-wide commitment to the project management culture. The emphasis is to ensure that project management supports the business goals of the organization. Therefore, detailed quantitative measures of effectiveness of project management are collected and used by upper management. Quantitative project objectives are set to measure progress in implementing project management procedures and to determine the effectiveness of these procedures. In level-four organizations, project success is more uniform, partially because project management is recognized as a professional core competency. In addition, performance in the areas of quality, cost, and schedule conform to the plan. Figures 5.4 and 5.5 contain tables that allow one to summarize the effectiveness of the project procedures in the individual facets of project management and for each element of the project life cycle.

At level four, the PMO assumes greater responsibilities as it coordinates project management initiatives organization-wide and assesses the contribution of project management to the organization. The PMO takes the lead

	Process	Compliance	Efficacy
Scope, 1–5	√	√	√
Quality, 1–5	√	√	√
Cost, 1–5	√	√	√
Schedule, 1–5	√	√	√
Contract, 1–5	√	√	√
Risk, 1–5	√	√	√
Integration, 1–5	√	√	√
Reporting, 1–5	√	√	√
Team, 1–5	√	√	√
Client, 1–5	√	√	√
Vendor, 1–5	√	√	√
Communcation, 1–5	√	√	√
Overall Project Performance, 1–5	—	—	—

Figure 5.4 Organizational Project Management: Maturity Assessment

	Inception	Planning	Implement	Close-Out
Scope, 60	√	√	√	√
Quality, 40	√	√	√	√
Cost, 40	√	√	√	√
Schedule, 40	√	√	√	√
Contract, 40	√	√	√	√
Risk, 40	√	√	√	√
Integration, 30	√	√	√	√
Reporting, 30	√	√	√	√
Team, 70	√	√	√	√
Client, 30	√	√	√	√
Vendor, 30	√	√	√	√
Communication, 50	√	√	√	√
Overall Performance, 500	—	—	—	—

Figure 5.5 Life-Cycle Organizational Maturity Assessment

in establishing quantified project objectives to improve project management performance and in monitoring the performance in meeting these objectives. The PMO collects information to be used to determine the value of project management, and to ensure that project management supports the organization's business goals. The PMO also collects information on the status of the organization's best practices in project management. The PMO leads the organization's efforts to determine which of the potential projects the organization should pursue.

Another key responsibility at level four that the PMO performs is to coordinate resource use through the integrated management of projects and the coordination and management of multiple, related projects. The PMIS at this level interfaces with the organization's accounting, financial management, and human resource management systems. Stakeholders, including clients and vendors, can access the PMIS directly on individual projects.

With the emphasis on quantitative objectives and on assessing the value of project management to the organization, knowledge management will take on an increased emphasis. For example, the PMO establishes a link from a project's WBS dictionary to the organization's knowledge management system. Then, to ensure that the needs of the entire organization are met, the PMO regularly reviews the classification system for scope changes. For the purpose of comparisons across projects, the PMO establishes a facilitative method for documenting cost estimates. In the area of risk management, the PMO provides the following guidance: evaluation of threshold criteria for action, risk scoring and interpretation methods, checklists for risk identification and analysis, and a description of qualitative and quantitative risk analysis techniques. The PMO serves as the focal point for project management activities so that information about make-or-buy costs are compared to costs on previous procurements as part of the decision-making process. The PMO collects data on the effectiveness of the use of various types of procurement documents, contracts, and supplier performance indices.

The PMO leads the organization in the use of advanced techniques in time management, such as critical chain and reverse resource allocation scheduling. Other advanced techniques include integrated earned value analysis, use of earned value as a tool for risk monitoring and control, quality function deployment, complex cost-estimating models, and methodical configuration management.

At level four, project management is considered a core competency in the organization. Accordingly, the PMO leads this effort as it establishes objectives to improve project management capabilities throughout the organization. The PMO also establishes a project management career path and uses a competency model in conjunction with proficiency charts. These competency tools enable succession planning so that key resource requirements are known. It also establishes an internal certification program for project professionals. Working in partnership with the human resources management unit, the PMO establishes a personal development plan for use by each individual in project management. This plan facilitates the determination of each person's contribution to the overall project objectives and to the organization's strategic goals. To support individuals as they move up the project management career path, the PMO establishes and coordinates a mentoring program for individuals and project teams. Specific goals are established for program participants.

5.2.5 Level Five

Level five is described as optimizing with a focus on continuous improvement. In level-five organizations, project management roles and responsibilities are well understood, and there are organizational objectives for improvements in project management. Project management procedures are regularly fine tuned to achieve organizational objectives. Common causes of project management problems are prioritized and systematically eliminated. There is participation in benchmarking forums as a way to continue to generate ideas for improvement and as a way to refine project performance metrics. In these organizations, continuous improvement of the project management process is enabled by timely feedback on project cost and schedule performance and by fostering innovative ideas and technologies. Further, in level-five organizations, project success is the norm, and projects meet, or surpass, objectives in the areas of cost, schedule, scope, and quality. In these organizations, it is recognized that projects depend on successful and effective processes, that projects are a reason for success, and that projects are an integral part of the business.

The level-five PMO is responsible for a project management improvement plan with quantitative objectives for project management improvement, resource requirements, and training needs. For people to understand the importance of these initiatives, the PMO provides training in continuous improvement because this is an expected area of emphasis for each individual. The PMO seeks proposals from people at all levels in the organization for improvement initiatives. In turn, the PMO provides recognition to those who support this improvement program. At the end of each project, the PMO formally measures customer satisfaction. The PMO serves as the organization's representative in external communities of practice, such as project management knowledge networks. The PMO coordinates and integrates resource planning, resource acquisition, and resource assignment. As part of this process, the PMO provides forecasts for use in human resource management as project portfolio teams conduct project selection and prioritization. Thus, the PMO facilitates enterprise resource forecasting, planning, and integrated decision making. Working in partnership with customers and suppliers, the PMO ensures an integrated team support for each project.

5.2.6 A Rank of Zero

What is graciously missing from these rankings is the rank of zero, which describes an organization that has no procedures, and none of its projects is ever near the success mark. One hopes that such an organization does not exist, although it is possible for an organization to merit a ranking of zero on one of the performance attributes. If that turns out to be case, then the improvement plans that usually follow a maturity assessment will have development of project processes and procedures as the first priority.

5.3 METRICS RELATED TO MATURITY LEVELS

Specific characteristics of metrics can be tied to specific maturity levels in a project management maturity assessment (Levin, 1999; O'Hara and Levin, 2000). These characteristics are performance, stability, compliance, capability, and improvement (Florac et al., 1997).

5.3.1 Performance Metrics — A Level-Two Emphasis

Metrics in this category emphasize project performance by way of highlighting the ability to deliver products and services with the qualities, timeliness, and costs that customers require. If performance metrics vary erratically and unpredictably over time, the project management process is not in control of the project. With performance metrics, it is possible to assess repeatability of project management techniques, and to determine whether or not internal and external requirements are being met. These metrics basically gather specific facts, and they are not judgmental. By definition, their focus is on attributes of quality, quantity, cost, and time.

The key in determining specific metrics is to choose attributes or measures that are relevant to the specific project. These metrics usually relate to quality, resource consumption, or elapsed time. Then, as many product quality and process performance attributes as needed are measured, at several points in time. The choice of what to measure depends on the project at hand (see Figure 5.6).

5.3.2 Stability Metrics — A Level-Three Emphasis

Stability is central to any organization's ability to produce products and to deliver services according to plan. Stability also refers to the ability to improve processes with better and more competitive products and services as the end result. For example, if people in the organization are using the project management methodology, but products and services still are not meeting the customer's requirements, the methodology is not stable and must be improved to reduce the variability.

- Completeness of requirements
- The extent of the rework necessary to satisfy customer expectation
- Number of key milestones completed and number of key milestones missed
- Use of the WBS to develop budgets, identify risks, and identify resource requirements
- Use of the project charter effectively to manage and resolve authority and responsibility conflicts
- Accuracy of the cost estimate as compared with actual costs at the project and work package level
- Expected results and actual results in testing
- Resource utilization vs. the plan
- Extent of the requests for information outside of regular communications
- Effectiveness of risk response strategies in terms of mitigating risks
- Vendor progress in terms of meeting schedule, cost, and performance

Figure 5.6   Examples of Performance Metrics

For stability metrics, an attribute is measured, and its value is tracked over time. If measurements fall outside the range of prescribed acceptable variation, the process may not be stable. If processes are stable, the metrics still may vary in known nonrandom ways, but the variations may be due to common causes or normal variations of the process, which exist because of normal interactions among people and other resources (see Figure 5.7).

5.3.3 Compliance Metrics — A Level-Three Emphasis

For project management to be stable and predictable, it must be used consistently in the organization. Compliance means that the standards of knowledge and practice of project management exist within the organization, and that they are followed. Compliance assesses adherence to the process; fitness and use of people, tools, technology, and procedures; and

- Effectiveness of schedule and cost tracking and controlling process with the value of the scheduling and costing tools and techniques in managing projects
- Effectiveness of the contract change management system
- Revisions to the subsidiary plans of the overall project plan, such as the procurement, cost, or quality management plan

Figure 5.7   Examples of Stability Metrics

fitness and use of support systems. Project management processes that are clearly defined, effectively supported, faithfully executed, reinforced, and maintained point to project management maturity and are more likely to be stable, repeatable processes. For this to be the case, project personnel must be aware of, trained in, and given the tools needed for proper execution of these processes.

Mature project management depends on consistent execution of the process. The methodology must be executed exactly as defined. For example, although an organization may have a PMO, the latest project management software, a methodology, project mentors, a project management training program, and a project management career path, there is no guarantee that people in the organization actually use the project management concepts, tools, and techniques. The issue to be examined is the penetration of project management practices across an organization. One must determine to what extent project management practices are being used. Measurements involving compliance do not address performance per se. Their purpose is to provide information to help explain performance results, variations, and patterns that are observed. Metrics can detect and diagnose what actually is under way (see Figure 5.8).

5.3.4 Capability Metrics — A Level-Four Emphasis

The capability metric helps predict the quality of products. This metric is a necessary characteristic in determining if project performance has satisfied customer requirements, and in assessing whether project performance has met business needs. Any variations must fall within ranges that are mandated for business success.

- Applicability of the methodology for the range of projects under way in the organization
- Product conformance with requirements
- Effort required to use the PMIS and timeliness of its information
- Customer acceptance of product deliverables
- Extent of tools and templates provided by the PMO
- Extent of changes to the cost baseline
- Need for tailoring the organization's quality policy to fit specific projects
- Number of workarounds required
- Conflicts between the project manager and the contracts manager that require escalation

---

Figure 5.8 Examples of Compliance Metrics

- Extent to which project work is integrated within the organization
- Benefit of project work to the organization
- Status of the organization's best practices in project management
- Use of models for schedule, cost, and performance
- Capability and ease of use of the organization's integrated systems
- Use of knowledge, skills, and competency profiles
- Participation in the project management career path
- Participation in mentoring programs
- Extent of improvement of project predictability

Figure 5.9   Examples of Capability Metrics

Project management should have predictable results. If so, the project management processes are termed capable. Analysis of performance then can identify areas where the capability of a process can be improved for more effective support of business objectives. Capability may need to be improved to satisfy competitive pressures or to comply with customer needs. Most of these metrics must be collected through interviews with project personnel or through periodic surveys (see Figure 5.9).

5.3.5   Improvement Metrics — A Level-Five Emphasis

Improvement metrics focus on the performance of the project management process. The emphasis is on how project management can help move the organization to a level of greater profits, how to determine if project management is working successfully throughout the organization, and if the recent changes that have been introduced were effective. To promote improvements, people must understand the business goals and strategies of the organization. People must also be cognizant of the priorities, risks, and issues associated with these goals and strategies. Improvement metrics thus must correspond with business indicators. The costs and benefits of project management improvement must relate to the business indicators used in the organization (see Figure 5.10).

- Impact of each improvement proposal in terms of increasing capability in one of the project management competencies
- Effect of technology in terms of performance improvement
- Individual involvement in performance improvement initiatives

Figure 5.10   Examples of Improvement Metrics

5.4 THE PMO AND METRICS

In establishing a metrics program, the PMO should take the lead by identifying the key project and process management issues, by selecting and defining the corresponding measures, and by integrating the measures into existing processes. Data should not be collected unless they will be used.

Definitions and context descriptions should be retained, together with direct measurement data. Methods of analysis and interpretation of the collected information must be carefully described. Methods to detect real concerns rather than normal variations are required. Inferences must be drawn from data to guide decisions and actions. The PMO should design methods, and obtain tools, to support data collection and retention. The PMO then should train staff in data collection procedures, making the data collection process as easy as possible. Data are collected as a basis for action, so the data must be captured and stored for subsequent analysis, which should lead to suggestions for improvement in project processes.

The PMO must ensure that people in the organization recognize that the metrics are being collected as part of an initiative in project management improvement intended to improve the effectiveness of processes and the quality of products. Clearly understood factual data facilitate correct analysis; they also help ensure there is agreement on what is happening and what should be happening. Metrics can form the basis of such clear, objective communication with project stakeholders.

5.5 PROJECT MANAGEMENT MATURITY ASSESSMENT

The project management maturity assessment is the foundation for continuous improvement in project management practices. The project management maturity assessment identifies the organization's project management strengths and weaknesses, and it quantifies the effectiveness of the organization's past efforts to improve project management capability. An assessment provides a means by which one can benchmark the organization's project management capabilities with capabilities of other organizations. Further, a comprehensive assessment should identify and prioritize the steps an organization needs to take to improve its project management capability. In turn, the project management procedures that are modified in response to the assessment will hopefully effect improvements in project performance, employee morale, and organizational cost effectiveness (Figures 5.11 and 5.12).

Figure 5.13 shows the steps that must be followed during an assessment. First, the organization should be committed to the idea of a maturity model and to using an assessment for project management improvements.

- ■ Guide PM improvements
- ■ Communicate the need for change
- ■ Help to promote buy in and commitment
- ■ Improve and develop competitive position
- ■ Promote enterprise project management

Figure 5.11   Using Assessments

- ■ Guide advancement
- ■ Identify deficiencies
- ■ Provide the foundation on which to build improvements

- ■ NOT:
  - ■ Provide a quick fix for projects in trouble

Figure 5.12   Maturity Assessment Focus

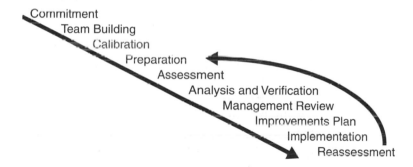

Commitment
Team Building
Calibration
Preparation
Assessment
Analysis and Verification
Management Review
Improvements Plan
Implementation
Reassessment

Figure 5.13   Maturity Model Process

The organization requests that an assessment be done, rather than having it imposed externally, such as often is the case in an audit. The scope of the assessment must be determined clearly. It must be clarified whether the assessment will include all aspects of project management or only certain areas such as risk management or procurement management. Another issue to clarify is whether the assessment will include all departments and divisions in the organization or only certain units. Finally, plans must identify the projects that will be part of the data gathering and the project professionals who will be interviewed for their perspectives on organizational project management capability.

The people who will be part of the assessment must prepare for the task. This generally is done through a kick-off meeting explaining the purpose of the assessment, each person's role, and how the results are to be used throughout the organization (Lubianinker and Levin, 2001). Then, data are collected, analyzed, and verified with the people in the organization who are sponsoring the assessment (Figure 5.13). The final deliverable of an assessment is an improvement plan, with a prioritized action list, that highlights what should be done so that the organization can continue to advance its project management capabilities (Levin et al., 1999). The recommendations in this plan are then implemented, and later, a reassessment is conducted to determine whether the desired changes have occurred in practice in the organization.

The sources of data for an assessment are project managers, project team members, project sponsors, support functional managers, customers, vendors, and project management office staff. The assessment process involves collecting project data, which is categorized by the project's dollar size, strategic importance, complexity, geographic location, and stage in the life cycle. The survey instruments include questionnaires, interviews, and review of project-specific documents in order to develop quantified and summarized indicators for each project management facet. In addition, organizational documents, such as project management methodologies, policies, and procedures, are reviewed.

The overall organizational ranking is a summary of the divisional rankings. In turn, organizational rankings are summaries of rankings for quantitative facets and qualitative facets of project management across all divisional projects. A maturity ranking highlights organizational commitments, and strengths and weaknesses of the organization.

The results of a maturity assessment usually provide organizational perspectives, incentives to focus on causes of problems, and the consequences of inadequate or nonexistent procedures (Figure 5.14). Therefore, the recommendations generated as part of an assessment process would highlight improvement of the organizational areas in the context of project management knowledge areas and with attention to the organizational infrastructure for project management. The assessment should provide a guidebook describing which improvements should be undertaken first. Since these improvements are tied to the assessment itself, the assessment findings help communicate the need for changes to the rest of the organization, promote a commitment for the improvement initiatives, and heighten project management visibility.

5.6 THE ROLE OF THE PMO IN MATURITY ASSESSMENT

It is very difficult to *consistently* deliver quality products and services to customers if project management processes are ineffective. Improving processes results in a corresponding improvement in products and services. Typically, the PMO serves as the lead in the assessment and as the

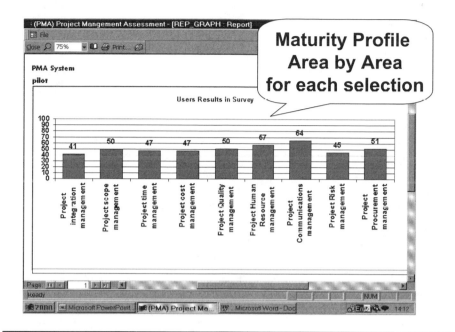

Figure 5.14 PMA Sample Report

focal point for the process. Therefore, the PMO will be responsible for implementing the project management improvement program based on the assessment results. Each recommendation from the assessment should be considered an opportunity for improvement.

Each recommendation should be considered as a small project. For each project, a short proposal should be prepared that describes the current situation, the proposed change, who will benefit, who will be responsible, and the estimated costs, resources, and schedule. The PMO should coordinate each of these improvement projects. It should also assign responsibility to ensure that implementation does in fact occur. This cannot be considered part-time work, which is to be done in one's spare time after the real work is done; it must be considered a priority assignment.

The PMO must also identify the most critical problems. The PMO should then develop a prioritized process improvement strategy and phased implementation plan because not all projects can be done at once. This can be done by assessing the business impact, the critical success factors, and the risks by examining how each proposed project can help the organization achieve the next level in the maturity model. First, in light of the organization's business objectives and critical success factors, one must assess the impact on the proposed project against the ongoing strategic business objectives of the organization. The PMO should assess the risks of each improvement project to determine the difficulty that is involved. Determination of difficulty is based on the answers to the following questions:

- Is the proposed change easy to implement, such as a requirement for all projects to have formal closeout plans, or difficult, such as a requirement for every project in the organization to follow a standard, consistent methodology that has not yet been developed?
- Are there technology risks, and will new tools be required that also necessitate training?

Next, one should consider structural areas such as the number of groups in the organization that must be involved, the people required to develop the solution, and the level of resistance to change. For example, many organizations must be involved if a standard project management methodology is to be developed and implemented. By comparison, only the human resources unit and the PMO would need to be involved if the project involved training in project management software. Each project should be assessed in terms of its ability to enable the organization to achieve the next level in the maturity rating scale. The process improvement plan should be submitted to senior management for concurrence and commitment and to promote buy-in throughout the organization.

Analogous to how a PMO can assist the recovery of a runaway project and improve its performance, a PMO can help the organization achieve a higher maturity rating. The latter is achieved by developing a clearinghouse of best practices, by integrating these best practices into the planning and implementation of all projects, by providing training for the project personnel, and by indoctrinating the upper management.

In today's competitive marketplace, a strategy of continuous improvements in organizational products, services, and processes is required to survive and grow. Project teams are the principal means by which organizations marshal the resources of the enterprise to bring about continuous improvements in those things of value created for customers and other stakeholders. The emergence and use of project management processes and techniques are significant management improvements. Projects then become the building blocks in the design and execution of organizational strategy. Those projects whose objective is to bring about continuous improvement to products, services, and processes are important building blocks in preparing the enterprise for its competitive future. Lasting change requires constant effort. Therefore, the PMO, by serving as the focal point for the project management improvements, can ensure that maturity will be sustained.

CONCLUSIONS

The organizational project management maturity model measures the ability of the collective organizational project management staff to deliver projects on time, according to specifications, and within budget. Generally, maturity models use a scale of 1 to 5. Higher maturity levels signify more effective project procedures, higher quality deliverables, lower project costs, higher project team morale, and improved profits for the organization. Lower maturity models characterize organizations that repeatedly experience failed projects, implement redundant procedures, and have a history of misdirected improvement efforts.

6

FUNCTIONS OF THE PMO

6.1 OVERVIEW

There are many descriptions for the functions of a PMO. The primary reason is that this concept is evolving, and therefore some descriptions tend to be outgrowths of the previous descriptions. As noted by Project Management Institute in the *PMBOK® Guide*, "There is a range of uses of what constitutes a project office." It operates on a continuum, from providing support functions for project managers to being responsible for the results of the project (Project Management Institute, 2000a, p. 21). Descriptions thus focus on different aspects of the PMO functions. As stated by Casey and Peck (2001), "PMO means vastly different things to different people with only this as their consistent thread: Something that's going to fix our project management mess" (p. 40).

There is a movement in many organizations to consider the PMO in terms of a series of levels, in the same vein as a project management maturity model. Here, a level-one PMO might support just one project, a level-two PMO would support several projects under the same program, a level-three PMO would support a division or department in the organization with all of its projects, a level-four PMO would support the organization in its projects, and a level-five PMO would be placed strategically at an executive level and would support business strategy decisions and resource allocations at the enterprise level (Figures 6.1–6.4). At level five, the PMO is comparable to the description of its functions in PMI's Program Management Office Specific Interest Group (http://www.pmi.org/sigs/pmo) "The organizational structure, its methodologies, processes, procedures, controls, tools, people, training, and all necessary components required to integrate existing projects, manage the portfolio, control the required functions, and successfully deliver an organization's business objectives." This chapter describes the full set of PMO functions.

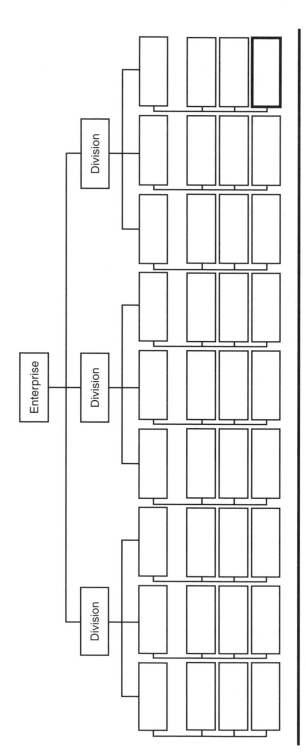

Figure 6.1   Area of Project Coverage

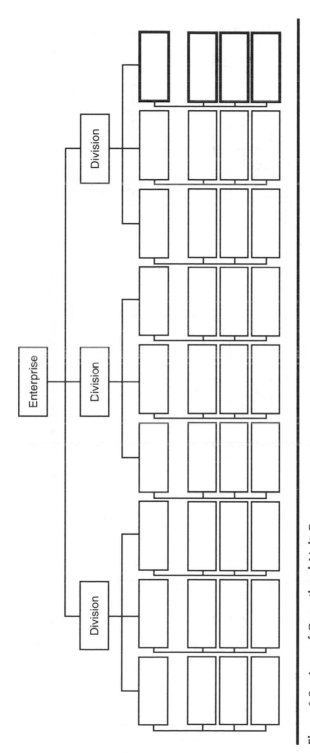

Figure 6.2   Area of Operational Unit Coverage

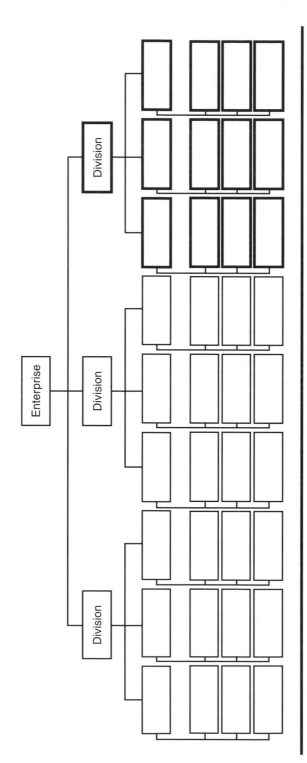

Figure 6.3 Area of Divisional Coverage

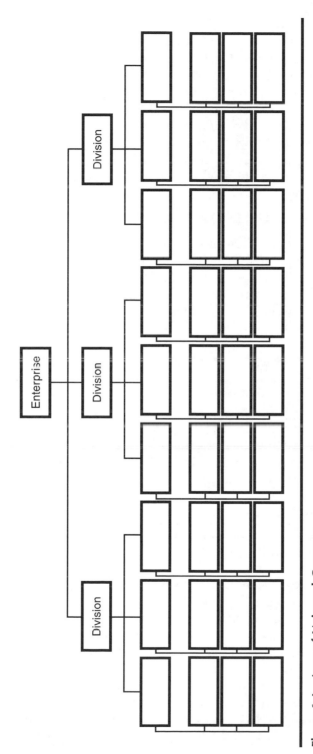

Figure 6.4 Area of Universal Coverage

Probably the most widely used description of functions are those that assist projects. If these are complemented by organization-oriented functions, then the resulting PMO will be an exceptionally effective unit in achieving project management maturity, and more importantly, in facilitating higher profits and in maintaining the competitive advantage of the organization. The PMO then essentially acts as the interface between the project managers and the organization. Even at this point, the PMO can change the entire direction of the organization to one in which there is enterprise project management. Alternatively, the organizational goals and needs might dictate adoption of only a small set of these functions.

6.2 PROJECT-FOCUSED FUNCTIONS

Augmentation is the most direct route for improving project performance in that the PMO will provide personnel to the project for the performance of certain tasks. Mentoring is the process by which PMO personnel work together with project personnel to ensure proper execution of certain tasks. Finally, consulting is the process by which the PMO provides occasional problem-solving ideas (Figure 6.5). The misplaced haste and unplanned fast pace that is normally imposed on projects often advances augmenting, mentoring, or consulting as substitutes for training. Formal training is the next logical step, in the unlikely event that the urgency of the project's missions allows such excursions.

```
■ Augment
   ■ Fill the gaps in team resources
■ Mentor
   ■ Work side by side with novice team members
■ Consult
   ■ Provide occasional validation and assistance
```

Figure 6.5   Project-Focused Functions

The PMO provides mentoring and establishes consulting services in all areas of project management. Mentoring and consulting efforts allow current project team members to perform satisfactorily for the benefit of the project at hand. By comparison, training enhances the general competence of the organization, and improves the effectiveness of future project managers, if in fact there is sufficient time to train the project manager and team members. The areas of coverage of these activities will be planning, estimating, scheduling, risk management, people management, and general assistance in implementing the project (Figure 6.6). Proper use of appropriate software for each of the project phases will be included in these PMO functions.

	Consult	Mentor	Augment
Scope	√	√	√
Quality	√	√	√
Cost	√	√	√
Schedule	√	√	√
Risk	√	√	√
Integration	√	√	√
Change	√	√	√
Contract	√	√	√
Communication	√	√	√
Team	√	√	√
Client	√	√	√
Vendor	√	√	√

Figure 6.6   Project-Focused PMO Functions

The PMO should establish guidelines for company-wide competencies, project-specific skills, and situational crisis management tools. These guidelines are used when it is determined that PMO personnel will be involved in recovery of a project. The PMO and the project team will jointly agree if a mentoring, consulting, or augmenting relationship will be useful and/or necessary. The PMO and the project team will define the basic elements of this relationship, including the expected benefit of the relationship, the level of direct involvement of the PMO staff in the project, immediate goals, project goals, and major milestones. In addition, the agreement will include details on frequency of contact, duration of each session, and responsibilities of each party. As the starting point, a matrix such as the one shown in Figure 6.6 should be used to map the areas and modes and assistance that should be expected of the PMO.

The project-focused functions generally have a short-term impact on the project, even if they are provided by the PMO, although ideally the PMO should be focused primarily on the long-term project management missions of the organization. Project-focused functions are intended to have immediate impact on the performance of the project, and they are usually for remedial purposes. More often than not, project-focused functions are the only ones that are available to the project managers by way of assistance and facilitation through an abbreviated form of the PMO, which is sometimes called the Project Office. The solutions provided by this category of functions are instant, with almost immediate results. As noted by Bernstein (2000), the PMO serves to provide support to the project manager so that the project manager can focus on delivering the goals and objectives of the project, on project execution, on timelines, and on deliverables. However, the fact cannot be overstated that the overall cost of providing such short-term facilitation is far more than providing proactive long-term solutions. In many ways, augmenting, mentoring, and consulting are time critical, and therefore they are akin to crisis management.

6.2.1 Augment

Augmentation is the process by which the PMO serves in a fashion somewhat similar to a "temporary" agency in that it provides personnel of various skills to the project in order to fill any shortfalls that might exist in the project staff. If the full complement of a PMO exists in the organization, then these temporary project staff members will also serve as a conduit for best practices and company policies into the project. Otherwise, they simply serve as additional resource hours for the project manager.

In properly managed organizations, success depends on how effectively resources are used. If an organization does not have a formal resource allocation process, project managers are left on their own to solicit and obtain resources from functional managers. This situation only leads to conflicts and difficulties that will hamper the project team's efforts in completing the project successfully. Therefore, the PMO should provide resource management capabilities across the organization. The PMO can serve as a resource pool for project professionals. It is only then that resource requirements can be balanced across projects. Building on the knowledge, skills, and competency profiles, the PMO can assign project managers to specific projects in their areas of expertise. It can make decisions on the best use of an organization's resources to meet its goals.

6.2.2 Mentor

Mentoring occurs when the project has the right number of staff members, but the team members do not possess the appropriate competency to carry out their respective project duties. In such a circumstance, the PMO assigns a seasoned professional to assist and work with those project team members who have shortfalls in their competencies. The mentor will work side by side with the team member for as long and as often as necessary until such time that the team member and/or the project manager feel comfortable that the team member can perform his or her functions without direct intervention by the PMO staff member. A graceful way of phasing out of a mentoring arrangement is to convert it to a consulting arrangement, where the contact meeting is on an as-needed basis.

6.2.3 Consult

Consulting is the mode of assistance of choice when the team members feel comfortable performing most of their project-related duties, although they would like the comfort of validating the correctness of analysis, and the viability of assumptions, with a seasoned professional. Again, one would hope that, as the team becomes more competent and as the team's comfort level is elevated, the consultancy incidents will be minimized.

It is an important point that, at both the project and organizational levels, the key PMO functions involve augmenting, mentoring, and consulting. The difference is the extent to which the PMO participates in project performance. The functions to be performed are based on the goals and objectives of the PMO.

6.2.4 Areas of Assistance

The following is a representative, although not an exhaustive, list of project tasks that will become the subject of direct project assistance by the PMO.

6.2.4.1 Establish Standards for Managing Projects

If the organization does not have a standard project management methodology in place, each project team must determine the specific procedures it plans to follow and the tools it will use. This set of procedures constitutes the majority of the planning phase of the project.

The PMO can provide assistance by setting up basic project standards that are to be followed on each project. This includes a project life cycle to define the beginning and end of each project in specific terms. Other planning and implementation assistance include outlining the technical work to be done in each phase; developing a procedure to guide project teams in the preparation of detailed project plans; preparing standard forms and templates; and formulating a process that describes which people in the organization must review and sign off on project plans and other documents.

When the organization has a consistent and common approach to managing its projects, then each project can proceed more effectively and efficiently. And, with a consistent process in place, it also will be easier for project professionals to move from one project to another, since there will be a common frame of reference concerning project management in the organization.

To ensure that the common methodology is followed, the PMO must audit projects periodically and use the results of these audits to improve the standard methods as a result of experience. Each project will have ideas and lessons to share. The PMO incorporates new approaches into its standard methodologies. By building upon these lessons learned, successful projects will eventually become the norm and not the exception.

This process should consist of a set of core tasks that should be performed on each project. Some projects may have additional tasks that must be done in order to meet unique requirements or various tasks imposed by customers. For each task, different activities must be performed to ensure project success. Recognizing that some projects may not require the same level of detail as others, the PMO can develop criteria for scalability of the methodology requirements based on the type of project and the nature of the technical work to be done, the resource requirements, and the project duration.

Although each project is unique and differs in some way from other projects that are under way or previously completed in the organization, standard templates can assist in project management. As part of the development of the project management methodology, the PMO can develop standard templates for items such as the project plan, work breakdown structure, resource breakdown structure, and the activity list. These standard templates can then be used in projects of any type and complexity. Building on the commonalities of projects in the same organization, many of these standard tools can be reused from one project to another.

6.2.4.2 Standardize Report Forms

Reporting on projects is a mandatory activity. Reports provide stakeholders with information about how resources are being used to accomplish project objectives. Reports must contain information as to the status of the project in terms of its plans. Reports may be designed as summaries, or as a detailed description of a particular task or activity or some other element of the project. The intended readership of these reports may be the performing organization, the customers, or users.

Typically, if the organization does not have a PMO, each project has its own reporting system, and it is up to the project manager and the team to spend time to develop the reporting formats for each project. In immature organizations, reports are prepared as a response to special requests. However, although different stakeholders request similar information, they may want it reported at different times and in different formats. Under these circumstances, the project team may feel that its major mission is responding to requests for information. Furthermore, with reporting done on an individual basis on each project, it is difficult at the organizational level to compare progress across projects, or to determine the impact of each project on the total business objectives.

The PMO can provide assistance to projects by establishing standardized report forms for use on every project and by specifying the internal reporting requirements and the timing for the internal reports. This includes a standard method for reporting project status and for forecasting future progress, while still enabling each individual project to report information relative to the unique needs of its project stakeholders.

The PMO can also set up an internal organizational distribution system for reports. By establishing a common reporting process throughout the organization for use on all projects, the PMO can facilitate and encourage honest, timely, and accurate reporting at all levels. Such practices can spark interest in the reports so that the recipients will put the report information to good use, rather than discarding the report.

6.2.4.3 Select, Operate, and Support Project Management Software

A variety of software tools are available to support project management. Selecting the right tool or set of tools to use is important. These tools range from enterprise project management tools to those designed for a specific application, such as configuration management, project scheduling, requirements management, resource utilization, and cost estimating. The sophistication of many of these tools requires specialized training to install and operate. Regardless, for the software to benefit the project, the software must be properly installed, and its data must be current, reliable, and available.

The PMO staff can take responsibility for software selection, operation, and maintenance. Standard tools throughout the organization can facilitate the performance of project management activities. By standardizing the tools to use throughout the organization, it becomes easier to analyze data on projects, to exchange data on projects, to minimize duplicate data entry, and for people to move to another project elsewhere in the organization. To facilitate information exchange, interdependencies between projects can be identified, monitored, and facilitated.

The PMO can also provide funding for software acquisition, so that this is not a charge to each project in the organization. The PMO staff can be trained in use of the software and then can support each project team in installing the software, initially populating the data base, keeping the system up to date, preparing reports, and distributing reports to stakeholders.

6.2.4.4 Define and Implement Proposal Development Methodology

A strategic process is required that focuses on evaluating possible proposals, determining which ones to pursue, making decisions, and developing the actual proposal. The PMO can establish the process and also can provide support in terms of pink or red team reviews, prior to submission of the proposal to the customer. This process includes defining the elements of a proposal, defining the estimating models, and identifying appropriate parameters for the project estimate (or the bid, if the project is an external project); establishing bidding strategies and contract selection policies; and developing a standard proposal format, and methodologies for WBS development and resource breakdown structure development.

6.2.4.5 Draft Proposals

If a proposal development methodology already exists, then this task is a straightforward one comprised of following the guidelines already established. Otherwise, this task will include development of one-time standards for proposals and quickly putting a proposal together. It is an unfortunate fact of life that proposal turnaround time is always very short, and there is hardly ever enough time to leisurely conduct this task.

6.2.4.6 Provide Project Start-Up Assistance

Typically, the project manager is assigned at the end of the initiating phase of the project or during the early stages of the planning phase. Often, at the time the project manager is assigned, team members have not been selected, and the project manager must negotiate for resources with functional or departmental managers throughout the organization. Thus, much of project manager's time must be spent in resource negotiation and interface management.

Until the project team is fully staffed, the PMO can provide resources to support the project on an interim basis. These people can support the project manager by designing the information systems, defining the control systems, setting up the project workbook, establishing the war room or team room, preparing documents as required by the project management methodology, and providing overall staff support.

6.2.4.7 Prepare Project Charters and Scope Statements

In many organizations, project managers have responsibility and accountability for projects but lack the necessary authority to execute them. The project charter provides a clear and consistent definition of the project's mission, scope, and objectives. It also provides the project manager with the authority to apply organizational resources to the project objectives. Typically, the charter is prepared after the business case for the project has been made, and after the project has been approved.

Often, the project manager is not assigned to the project at the time the charter is prepared. Project Management Institute® in the *PMBOK® Guide*

(2000a) suggests that the project charter be issued by a manager external to the project at an appropriate level. The PMO is the most logical entity to develop a standard format to use for the project charter and to prepare the charter for each new project in the organization (see Appendix 6A). Once the sponsor signs and issues the charter, the PMO can distribute it throughout the organization. This charter can serve as an agreement between the sponsor and other managers who are at similar levels in the organization.

Similarly, the PMO can facilitate the process by developing a standard format for the scope statement for each project and by assisting in its development. A specific statement of the scope can help eliminate any confusion of stakeholder expectations throughout the life of the project. In addition, to manage stakeholder expectations during the project, a documented scope statement can be used throughout the project as a point of reference, particularly whenever scope changes are proposed.

6.2.4.8 Facilitate Project Kickoff Meetings

It has long been recognized that the kickoff meeting is critical to team building on any project, even on those projects in which the team members have previously worked together on similar, related efforts. During the kickoff meeting, the team members who will be involved on the project are brought together in a single location, perhaps for the first time. The kickoff meeting enables the team members to get to know one another, to establish working relationships and methods of communication, and to set specific team goals and operating procedures through the preparation of a team charter. The kickoff meeting is also an opportunity to review project goals, objectives, and plans, and to obtain individual and group commitments to the team (Stuckenbruck and Marshall, 1990, pp. 18–19).

To ensure that this meeting does not become a monologue by the project manager, the PMO staff can facilitate the meeting, while still allowing the project manager to chair it. In this way, the PMO facilitator can create a conducive atmosphere in which open-ended questions are asked, thus promoting uninhibited communication among the team members and the project manager, helping to relieve the anxieties of team members about their new assignments and roles, and helping to build a team climate. Having the PMO staff facilitate the session also shows support and commitment for the project at another level of the organization.

6.2.4.9 Conduct Project Risk Assessment

Managing risk is essential for project success and must be addressed throughout the project. High-quality data on project risks must be collected. As stated in the *PMBOK® Guide* (Project Management Institute,

2000a), risk management involves maximizing the probability and consequences of positive events to the project objectives, while minimizing the probability of adverse events (p. 127). Since the project manager is responsible for the overall risk management of the project, he or she will need additional specialized expertise and competency in the tools and techniques used in risk identification, analysis, response development, monitoring, and management.

The PMO can prepare a template for a risk management plan to use for each project. Such a template would help the team decide how best to handle risk management activities, and how to ensure that risk management has visibility at the project and organizational levels. The template also can help the team determine specific threshold criteria for risks. These thresholds specify the level of a specific risk that is acceptable to the organization, and the level at which action must be taken.

The PMO can identify, categorize, and analyze potential risks based on previous work in support of other projects in the organization, based on historical information of project files, and from published information that identify common sources of risk. Checklists and tables always promote consistency and uniformity. Therefore, the PMO should prepare checklists for use in identifying risks. If a Delphi approach is to be used to reach consensus on possible risks that may affect the project, the PMO can facilitate this process. The PMO staff can conduct interviews with people involved with the project to obtain their perspectives on risks. The PMO can assist the team in conducting risk probability and impact analysis and in using project simulation techniques such as Monte Carlo analysis.

Once risks have been identified, PMO staff members can support the project team in tracking and monitoring them. Additional areas of assistance include conducting risk response audits and risk reviews. With PMO involvement, a repository can be established containing risk management data for use throughout the organization as part of a knowledge management system.

6.2.4.10 Maintain Project Visibility Room

Whether the team is a collocated team or a geographically dispersed team, all project teams need to be able to share ideas, actions, and data. The sharing of ideas and data can take place in a physical location or a "war room," a "control room," a "project information room," or a "team room." Regardless of the form, this room serves as a location where members of the project team can meet, virtually or otherwise, to discuss problems. This room also serves as a place where project artifacts, records, and documentation can be maintained. The team room can provide meeting records and discussion forums, in paper form or in electronic form.

Information can be captured and stored in the project visibility room for all team members to see. This information can also serve as the historical information for the project. The purpose of this room is to ensure that everyone on the team then knows what is under way with the project. This room should be accessible to all project participants at any time. Therefore, accessing the information should be a simple process.

It is easy to set up such a site, but for it to have significant impact, it must be maintained properly. The PMO staff can assist the project team in establishing and maintaining this site and in keeping up-to-date information about the project's technical, cost, and schedule performance. The PMO staff also can provide training to new team members on how to use the site and on how to update information that is maintained at this site. A recent addition is the virtual room or the Web site for the project. The Web site can replace, or at least augment, many of the functions of the physical project room. It is very likely that the physical project room will be totally displaced by the Web site as a team room, particularly in the case of projects that are partially or totally located in different locations, and therefore, when the team is operating in the virtual mode.

6.2.4.11 Track and Record Changes Made to Project Requirements

As projects progress, change is inevitable, given the conflicting nature of the project objectives of meeting a schedule, to completing a project within budget, and delivering a product according to detailed specifications. Careful attention to each change is required so that the change only has a minimal impact on project delivery. As a result, it is imperative that the same change management process be used throughout the organization. Without such a plan and process in place, poorly managed changes can lead to schedule delays, excessive costs, low-quality deliverables, and decreased customer satisfaction.

The PMO can establish a classification system for project changes that can be used throughout the organization. The classification will define which changes need approval and from whom, and which changes the project manager can implement immediately. The PMO can prepare and distribute standard forms for use on all projects. Standard forms are used to request a change; to analyze the impact of this change on the project's objectives; to accept, defer, or reject the change; to communicate the change to project participants; and, when approved, to authorize its implementation. Project records also need to be updated to reflect the change. Procedures to monitor change are also required. Finally, on larger, more complex projects, the PMO staff can establish procedures describing the operation of a Change Control Board.

If the PMO establishes, and manages, an integrated change control process, the PMO staff can ensure that a change in one project that may affect another project, whether in terms of resources, schedule, or quality, is recognized and coordinated. By knowing the causes of changes that are encountered on a project, the PMO can support knowledge management in the organization. This support is manifested by assisting future projects in determining how best to react to a similar change and how to exert varying levels of influence.

6.2.4.12 Maintain Project Workbook or Library

Projects are paper intensive. For some projects, the creation and maintenance of documentation is a major cost item. Nevertheless, project documentation provides critical information to project participants. Each project requires a library of some type for its documents, including but not limited to items such as planning documents, requirements, specifications, user manuals, training materials, marketing materials, financial documents, memos and correspondence, and contractual and legal documents. Some of these items require formal control or configuration management. Therefore, all knowledge about the project should be part of the library (or workbook, in the case of small projects).

Effective project documentation supports the project management information system. Many project teams lack the luxury of a staff member who serves as the documentation manager or configuration manager. The PMO staff can provide this function in support of the project team. The PMO specifies retention and retrieval policies and procedures. The PMO establishes standard formats for the workbook or library for all projects and establishes methods for document control and configuration management.

6.2.4.13 Improve Accuracy and Timeliness of Timesheets

In many organizations, professionals working on projects do not report the time they spend on projects. Without time tracking, it is difficult, if not impossible, to obtain accurate information on the actual status of delivery predictions. An objective assessment of variance is not available, and accurate project costs at completion cannot be forecasted. In some cases, if time tracking is done, often it is only at the project level, not at a cost account or work package level. Each project also has its own informal accounting system in place that does not relate to the organization's system.

The PMO can provide assistance by establishing a standard format for reporting personnel time that is charged to each project. Such a centralized system is essential to ensure enterprise-wide resource planning, resource allocation, and cost accounting. The PMO can establish an electronic time sheet to be submitted, ideally on a weekly basis, to provide quick and accurate status information on all projects under way in the organization. This can facilitate the adoption of an organizational project-based accounting system, which in turn would lead to the development, implementation, and maintenance of integrated systems that would support the organization's management of its projects.

6.2.4.14 Administrative Assistance

The purpose of project control is to measure progress, monitor advancement toward objectives, evaluate what needs to be done to reach objectives, and take corrective or preventive action if necessary. As the project moves through its life-cycle stages, the PMO staff can help monitor and track performance. This involves project schedule maintenance, workbook/documentation maintenance, timesheet maintenance, budget tracking, etc. The PMO can review objectives against the plan and suggest needed changes before serious problems devlop. In order to keep the team spirit elevated, and the team members informed of the project activities, the PMO can publish a newsletter to be sent to all project stakeholders. The newsletter can be an informal one-page issue, or an elaborate multi-page multi-color rendition, depending on the size of the project.

6.2.4.15 Standardize Project Reviews

Project reviews are meetings held to assess the status and report the progress of the project. Reviews are required in order to determine whether or not projects should continue to receive resources. It is important to take a periodic look at the project from a strategic perspective to ensure that the project continues to provide support to the organization's mission, and to ensure that it is consistent with organizational strategy. At the end of each project, a final review should be conducted. This review is not used to assess performance in a negative fashion, but instead to provide an opportunity to objectively look back at the project, to reflect on experiences, to identify things that should have been done differently, and to identify other things that were done in a manner that should be repeated on future projects. A project that produces its desired product can also result in an improved process, and a list of recommendations for enterprise project management improvements.

For these reviews to be as effective as possible, a standard review format is required. Also helpful are a standard agenda, a detailed description of roles, and a clear definition of the responsibilities. The purpose of each review should be clear. The PMO staff can assist the project teams by preparing these review agendas with this standard format. Also, the PMO staff can help facilitate these reviews so that they are conducted in a neutral, objective way. The PMO staff can help encourage participation, ensure compliance with the standard agenda, and adherence to the prescribed starting time and ending time. The PMO staff also can prepare and distribute minutes of each review, including action items that were discussed.

6.2.4.16 Promote Issue Resolution

Unresolved questions, problems, concerns, or conditions that are not managed can have adverse effects on the project. Issues differ from risks, because issues result from events that have occurred. The extended project team, including customers and suppliers, must identify issues, and bring them to the attention of the project manager. Otherwise, issues can remain unresolved, and at times, these issues can cause a project to have unanticipated budgetary, schedule, or technical complications. It also is easy to forget a key issue in the face of other pressing concerns about the project.

The PMO can assist each project by developing and maintaining an issue evaluation and resolution process, and an issue management tracking system that will document issues in order to determine how to evaluate an issue, how to state the action items necessary to resolve them, how to communicate to the project team and to other affected projects in the organization regarding the issue, and how to formally close an issue. The PMO can also develop a method for prioritizing the issues, since some issues will be more important than others, and their action items will need a higher priority for accomplishment. In those situations in which the project team is unable to resolve an issue in a prescribed time frame, the project manager could escalate the item to the PMO for resolution. Such escalation is especially appropriate for high-severity issues, or even for low-severity issues that have been unresolved for some time.

The PMO can help identify trends or commonalities in issues across projects. Such information enables the organization to leverage on previous solutions for progress of future projects, by facilitating knowledge transfer on the issues that have surfaced, and those that were expected to surface and did not on previous projects.

6.2.4.17 Support Project Closeout

The closing phase of the project is typically the least exciting. At this point, the technical work of the project is done, and the remaining work involves obtaining final acceptance from the customer and completing administrative details. Since the project manager and the team are anxious to move on to other assignments, some key administrative requirements can be overlooked, such as the need to complete all project records, to return any customer-furnished equipment, to document lessons learned, and to archive records for future use in the organization. Closeout is admittedly a stressful time.

Some team members will have new assignments, while others will not, thus creating the grounds for interpersonal conflicts. Moreover, those persons who do not have a new and interesting assignment may wish to stretch out this phase of the project. Regardless, the closing phase represents a time of change for the project manager and all members of the project team.

The PMO can provide staff to assist in the closing process. To ensure nothing is overlooked, PMO staff can prepare a checklist of the tasks to be done during closeout. The PMO staff can provide administrative support to the project manager by providing a closeout manager to assist the project manager during this phase, and even to assume all of the duties of this phase if the project manager has a new assignment. This closeout manager then can ensure completion of all the project work, complete the documentation, and maintain the required records.

6.3 ENTERPRISE-ORIENTED FUNCTIONS

The PMO is the focal point for project management improvement and enhancement. This mission is met by establishing best practices and by providing training in all project management knowledge areas. It becomes the responsibility of the PMO to focus on areas such as development of lessons learned and standardized methodologies. The PMO serves as a facilitator, an enabler, and an advocate for improved performance across all projects in the organization. The PMO will continually define quantitative objectives for improving project management processes. It will maintain an extensive yet orderly archive of project performance data, together with an evolving list of lessons learned for all aspects of project management. The next natural step is to integrate and disseminate these best practices into the enterprise project management policies. Then, each project is considered as an opportunity for learning how to improve project processes and organizational approaches.

The PMO can provide easy-to-use and accurate models and procedures for estimates and schedules. It can provide and support enterprise-level project management tools for scheduling, resource management, time reporting, estimating, configuration management, requirements management, risk management, and a central repository for lessons learned.

Ultimately, the PMO can and should establish measurable objectives for continuous improvement of enterprise project management competence. It is crucial to develop organizational goals for the improvements in project management competence and then to compare the attained progress to the planned objectives. Essential in this process is the development of strategies for data collection, data refinement, data analysis, and reporting of the project performance results. In order to gauge the effectiveness of the project management activities, data will be collected to compare the progress in competence enhancement to its planning targets. To ensure that the organization obtains the best payback from its investment in professional project management, a continuous improvement program, with attention to lessons learned, can serve as the optimal formula for long-term organizational success.

6.3.1 Promote

Since the PMO is the focal point for project management enhancement, the best results will be obtained if the PMO personnel set objectives for such improvements and continually check the progress against the plans. In other words, the PMO must practice all of the monitoring and improvement philosophies that it prescribes for the projects. By publicizing such positive results on attaining its own goals, and hopefully the goals of all organizational projects, the PMO will continue to maintain a support base with the senior executives. Further, the upper management must be routinely briefed on project management principles and new developments in the profession, in order to integrate project management into the broader business context.

6.3.2 Archive

One of the more visible functions of a project management office is developing, recording, compiling, and disseminating the best practices in project management. This repository of information will be continuously evolving. The PMO will maintain project archives containing data on project life-cycle performance and project scope, cost, and schedule. On these facets of the project, data will highlight the original value, modifications, and the final value. Additionally, lists of issues and problems of previous projects will be available to all new projects. Thus, successive projects are able to build upon the lessons learned about previous projects.

Project data on scope, cost, schedule, quality, and risks must be collected, refined, and archived. Project documents on initial plans, change orders, and methods of change order approval also are required. Although these documents provide the starting point for data collection, the key is that the data, and/or their analysis, must be in a form that is accessible, reliable, and readily usable by future projects (Figures 6.7 and 6.8). Other data that must be distilled from the project progress information are the productivity of various specialties in crafting, developing, and assembling project modules.

6.3.3 Practice

It is not sufficient to collect project data and then to file that data away without guidelines as to how to best use it in future projects. A standard repository is required, which must be supported by each existing project.

- Promote
  - Advocate the PM culture by way of showing the tangible benefits of a corporate strategy
- Archive
  - Serves as a clearinghouse for project performance information
- Practice
  - Disseminate best practices and state-of-the-art procedures and guidelines
- Train
  - Provide ongoing training in all facets of PM

Figure 6.7   Enterprise-Oriented Functions

	Enterprise Oriented				Project Focused		
	Promote	Archive	Practice	Train	Consult	Mentor	Augment
Scope	√	√	√	√	√	√	√
Quality	√	√	√	√	√	√	√
Cost	√	√	√	√	√	√	√
Schedule	√	√	√	√	√	√	√
Risk	√	√	√	√	√	√	√
Integration	√	√	√	√	√	√	√
Change	√	√	√	√	√	√	√
Contract	√	√	√	√	√	√	√
Communication	√	√	√	√	√	√	√
Team	√	√	√	√	√	√	√
Client	√	√	√	√	√	√	√
Vendor	√	√	√	√	√	√	√

Figure 6.8   PMO Functions

In order to make data retrieval user friendly, the repository must be cross-referenced. Because the PMO is the organizational entity with exposure to multiple projects, it is in the best position to facilitate knowledge sharing through lessons learned. The PMO focuses on integrating positive project practices, promoting the use of recommended tools and templates, and providing guidance and support. Finally, these organizational experiences will form the basis of excellence for the parent organization, and as such, will be passed along to the project managers on a continual basis as part of the ongoing training programs, since they will be integrated into the enterprise project management policies and procedures.

Identify the project management competencies necessary for each project management function.

Develop a project position matrix for knowledge, skills, and competency analysis.

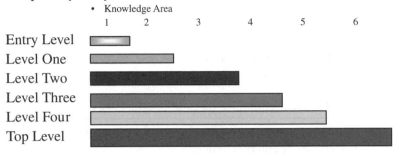

Figure 6.9 Competency Analysis

6.3.4 Train

The PMO is responsible for development and presentation of training modules on all aspects of project management. By giving this responsibility to the PMO, the organization demonstrates that professional development is both an individual and a corporate responsibility. The scheduling of personnel would be on a need basis in order to round out that particular team member's competency and not necessarily for the immediate benefit of the project at hand (Figures 6.9 and 6.10). If project evaluations indicate

	Inception	Planning	Implement	Close-Out
Scope	√	√	√	√
Quality	√	√	√	√
Cost	√	√	√	√
Schedule	√	√	√	√
Contract	√	√	√	√
Risk	√	√	√	√
Integration	√	√	√	√
Reporting	√	√	√	√
Team	√	√	√	√
Client	√	√	√	√
Vendor	√	√	√	√
Communication	√	√	√	√

Figure 6.10 Training Modules for Project Management Competency

shortcomings in some specific element of this matrix, additional training will be provided for that particular project team. Some organizations choose to provide training modules containing selected portions of the matrix to client and vendor representatives. Not everyone needs to be trained in all subjects. Training modules dealing with enterprise project management issues, such as project selection methods, multi-project resource management, or project management software evaluation, will be offered only to those team members who are, or are destined to become, part of the central PMO.

6.3.5 Areas of Performance

The following is a representative but not exhaustive list of enterprise-related tasks that the PMO should engage in at the enterprise level.

6.3.5.1 Estimating

Estimating is an essential function in project management and is performed throughout the project life cycle. Estimating determines the financial size of the project, the effort required in terms of resources, the schedule, and the cash flow to complete the project. Estimates form the basis by which later progress is assessed.

When estimating is performed at the PMO level, company-specific productivity history, company-specific learning curves, and appropriate experience curves can be applied to recurring tasks. The PMO can develop company-specific life-cycle cost and schedule models such as analogous models and parametric models. It will provide a working structure so that those developing estimates and schedules have access to a vast array of enterprise data contained in company-specific historical archives. The PMO will be in a good position to use the historical data to develop appropriate values for the parameters of the estimating models.

Beyond that, the PMO must maintain a portfolio of customized estimating models available for developing estimates at different points in the project lifecycle. These models include ratio models, analogous models, and power series models. Finally, the PMO must maintain organization-specific data on range estimates, learning curves, and experience curves.

6.3.5.2 Selection

For the sake of consistency, a standardized process of project selection and a set of common criteria are required for selection of projects to pursue. The PMO staff, serving as a neutral, objective forum, can best develop these criteria and this process. Projects link enterprise strategies to tangible results. Since there are not enough resources or assets to invest in every project, those projects that best support the organization's vision, mission, and goals must be selected. Further, even if the funds were available for all of the projects in the portfolio, too many projects under way at any one time would create the possibility that some related or unrelated projects may be at cross-purposes to one another. Project managers might lack access to needed resources and therefore will be unable to ensure cooperation from other organizational units. Frustration increases, and consequently many projects will be unsuccessful. It is more important to have fewer projects fully funded and staffed rather than a large number of projects under way that lack proper resource commitments.

Project selection should be based on organizational as well as project factors. Organizational factors include the organizational attitude toward projects and sophistication of the current information management systems. Project factors include the strategic importance of the project, size and complexity, budget, schedule, need for innovative skills, the value to the customer and end users, and the need to access a large and stable resource pool. The procedures for formalized project selection and project prioritization include identification of organizational priorities for projects, establishing metrics to evaluate priorities, developing project selection indices, managing a project portfolio, and assessing the current enterprise workload.

One approach to consider is for the PMO to group existing projects into categories, such as new product development, enhancement of existing products and services, process initiative, etc. Then, the PMO can establish goals in regard to organizational strategy for each category of projects. Each project can be aligned based on its contribution to organizational strategy. The PMO then can establish a framework for selection based on specific criteria for each category of projects and weights assigned to each criterion. This can be used to rank order projects that are to be pursued. Ideally, a mix of projects is recommended, consistent with business strategy.

The PMO can support and establish an executive level steering committee that would make final project selection decisions. In support of this committee, the PMO can perform a high-level assessment of the project's tangible and intangible benefits, and identify affected functional areas. Then, the PMO uses these data to develop and review alternative approaches for conducting the project. It can also determine the organizational impact if the project is not performed. The PMO can then recommend the most viable option to the executive selection committee. The PMO initiates project approval procedures so there is proper alignment with enterprise goals. The PMO follows a standard method to formally authorize project initiation. It should record which projects were ultimately selected and why. Once a decision is made to perform a project, the PMO will then communicate this decision to the project requester and the rest of the organization. The PMO should further document those projects that were not selected because of resource constraints but should be considered at a later time.

The PMO plays a major role in the periodic reprioritizing of projects based on changing business conditions. It can perform a review of all projects that are under way to ensure they are still contributing to organizational goals. The purpose is to identify those projects that might never have been formally closed out, and thus are still using valuable organizational resources without tangible results. The PMO can support "what if" analysis using various combinations of project portfolios to determine different views of cash flow analysis, return on investment, and resource requirements. As a result, some projects may need to be cancelled based on changing business conditions, or if total costs are higher than expected, or if resource consumption intensity exceeds initial expectations. The overall organizational objective is to have under way the most significant projects that are necessary for the organization to meet its strategic objectives. It is at this point that the organization's portfolio of projects is aligned in such a way that the contribution of project deliverables to the organization's objectives is maximized.

6.3.5.3 Data Integration

Many organizations manage a large number of projects simultaneously, but their project management information systems only provide visibility at the individual project level. Even when organizations have a consolidated reporting system, multiple project planning and reporting procedures may be unwieldy and difficult to use. Management reports then may be relatively meaningless since metrics may not be standardized across projects, and therefore inconsistent data are consolidated. This may be due to lack of consistency in planning and reporting standards, or to differences in documentation requirements across projects. Accordingly, the PMO must perform a leadership role in the area of data integration.

The PMO's data integration objectives are founded on a set of project procedures that are consistent with organizational business objectives. The goals of data integration will include standardizing project performance reports so that uniform data are collected for every project. The benefits of data integration include an efficient multi-project resource utilization environment through an integrated management policy. Data integration must use a common project management system in all projects. Such consistency will be achieved by using the same software system, the same data procedures, and the same data reporting system on every project that is implemented throughout the organization. Additional features of such a system would be developing working interfaces between the project cost and schedule management system, the organizational accounting system, and human resource management systems. The integrated data system will have utilities in cost estimate development, cost reporting, time sheet reporting, cost change management, and project progress reporting. It will enable tracking cross-functional, interproject dependencies.

The consistency should go beyond the software. That is, projects must use not only use the same software system, but also the same data collection procedures and the same data reporting procedures. Thus the project management information system should cut across organizational lines to capture the information needed for decision-making and to respond to potential opportunities as well as risks. This task is performed by documenting the effects of any changes in priorities, the consequences of changes in resource allocation, and the effects of adding additional projects to the organization's portfolio. Sharing information across projects can only lead to improvements in the quality of the decisions and enhancements in overall project success. It can disseminate the needed data from the PMIS to the users. The PMO can also provide training in the use of the data and related tools.

6.3.5.4 Reward and Recognition

Traditionally, organizations have a pay-for-performance approach in which each individual is rewarded based on his or her individual contributions. These systems encourage people to meet personal and professional goals first, even at the expense of project goals. Often, these systems tend to foster competition among team members, rather than cooperation and collaboration. A movement to a project-based organization may derail if there is no way to reward people for team efforts. According to Project Management Institute (2000a) in the *PMBOK® Guide*, the purpose of reward and recognition systems is to promote or reinforce desired behavior. The *PMBOK® Guide* further states that the link between project performance and reward should be clear, explicit, and achievable.

To highlight the importance of project work to the organization, the PMO can evaluate the organization's reward and recognition system and modify it to support a team-based system. It may be necessary to first set up separate systems for individual projects, and then to work to adapt a team-oriented, project-based system for the organization.

6.3.5.5 Project Audits

A PMO will have the appropriate resources to conduct regular and frequent project audits. The purpose of a project audit is to collect a series of data on all the various facets of the performance of ongoing projects. It can provide an impartial, objective appraisal of projects to establish their true status. Compiling and refining the data will provide a structured view of project performance. A project audit would identify best practices that can and should be transferred to other projects, as well as failed strategies that should be avoided in other projects.

The results of project audits and project closeout reports will be archived for use by PMO staff in defining future directions of the company. The archives will include data on scope, cost, and schedule of the project during the original, intermediate, and final stages of the project. Special archives can be dedicated to issues and problems that have occurred in the recent past and are likely to happen in the future.

The PMO can conduct a project audit several times during the project's life cycle, compile project data, refine the data to provide quantitative indicators of project performance, and use the project audit as a structured monitoring and review of the project performance. In this way, the project audit can be viewed as a useful tool for the project manager, rather than as a "gotcha game" (Levin, 1998). It can examine management of the project, methodology, procedures, budgets, expenditures, and the degree of completion. A timely audit can shed light on project errors so that they can be corrected.

The PMO also will prepare life-cycle cost models so that the cost of the project over the entire life cycle is determined, including not only development and implementation, but also operation, maintenance, and repair.

6.3.5.6 Facilitate Communication

Communication is critical to all PMO functions. To promote organizational change across organizational boundaries, the PMO facilitates communication on project management throughout the organization. This entity should be charged with keeping abreast of the latest developments in project management, and with implementing the latest best practices. The PMO can represent the organization at project management forums, meetings of professional organizations, and external knowledge networks.

6.3.5.7 Customer Satisfaction

Maintaining and tracking customer satisfaction is a responsibility of the project manager and is performed throughout the project at key deliverable milestones or testing points. However, the PMO can formally measure and track customer satisfaction on projects, for the benefit of the organization and toward continuation of business from the customer. The PMO can perform a final customer assessment during the closing phase. This customer satisfaction survey can be used as a way to gauge the level of value of the product or service to the customer. It can also use the results of this assessment to assess how well the collective organization is performing, and what needs to be done to enhance future project performance.

CONCLUSIONS

A PMO performs two different categories of functions: those that are project focused, short term, and remedial; and those that are enterprise oriented, long term, and visionary. The former includes augmentation of team resources, providing mentoring, and offering consulting to team members. The need for all of these functions arises from shortage of competent personnel and/or a lack of organization policy with respect to the projects. In the long run, the latter category of functions will obviate the need for the former set of functions. The enterprise-oriented functions include a forceful and logical advocacy for project management to the upper echelons of the organization, an effective and comprehensive archive of project performance data, a consistent and forceful application of the best practices as tempered by organizational history, and an ongoing training program for project personnel.

APPENDIX 6A
PROJECT CHARTER

Project Name		Project Number	
Project Manager	Phone	Fax	E-mail
Project Sponsor	Phone	Fax	E-mail
Customer	Address		
Objectives			
Scope			
Assumptions			
Constraints			
Major Risks			
Major Milestones			
Approvals:			
Project Manager	Signature		Date
Project Sponsor	Signature		Date
Department Manager #1	Signature		Date
Department Manager #2	Signature		Date
Department Manager #N	Signature		Date

7

IMPLEMENTING THE PMO

7.1 OVERVIEW

Implementing a PMO will facilitate improvements in the success of projects in the areas of scope, quality, cost, schedule, and customer satisfaction. A PMO will be commissioned to maintain the focus of the enterprise on both qualitative and quantitative facets of project management. With consistent tools and procedures and competent personnel who execute these integrated procedures, the organization will enjoy a higher rate of success in projects, which in turn will result in lower overall project costs, leading to increased corporate profits.

From organizational and client vantage points, the primary attributes that define the success or failure of a project are cost, schedule, scope, and client satisfaction. Projects must meet customer needs and respond to market conditions. They also must meet the business objectives that are established. A PMO will optimize the values of these success factors through development of consistent procedures and tools that are based on company-specific historical information, industry-wide best practices, and company-specific best practices. Mentoring, consulting, augmenting, archiving, promoting, clearing-housing, and training activities are functions that will ensure the dissemination and application of these skill and knowledge sets throughout the organization. The first three functions should become less intense as the PMO develops the project infrastructure for the organization.

7.2 MOTIVATIONS

The cost of establishing a fully developed PMO can be a major investment if the organization has never consciously attended to the needs of projects. On the other hand, organizations that are very sensitive to the success and performance of projects may not have to spend any appreciable additional amount of money establishing a formalized project management office. It is entirely possible that the capabilities described here as those of a PMO currently do exist in the organization, either separately or in the aggregate; they are just not called a PMO.

To use the designation of maturity models, if the projects of an organization all perform satisfactorily, and the performance continually gets better year by year, then the organization is at maturity level five, and therefore a very small investment is necessary for establishment of a formal PMO. The incentives for reaching level five are industry positioning with respect to best practices, the possibility of obtaining more business, and ultimately increased profits. These organizations have the ability to select and execute those projects that heighten the future success of the organization. On the other hand, if an organization must establish a PMO starting with the very basic elements, and with a sizeable investment, then the organization is probably at level-one maturity, which is the least sophisticated level (Figure 7.1). Here, investments in tools and processes are required to establish and roll out the PMO across the organization. Execution of several developmental stages are necessary to reap the full benefits from successful implementation of a PMO. Even with sizeable investments, it will take several years before progressive and sustained improvements are observed in organizational project performance. Nevertheless, by periodically repeating assessments, the PMO can benchmark the organization's current maturity level to industry standards and best practices, recognize areas in need of improvement, and demonstrate program effectiveness in terms of benefits and costs.

To keep the issues in perspective, there is an implicit cost in having a large number of failed projects. This implicit cost is significantly higher

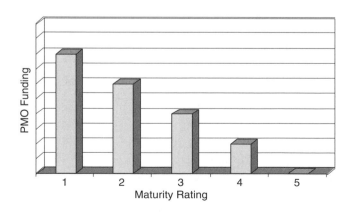

Figure 7.1 Additional Investment for PMO

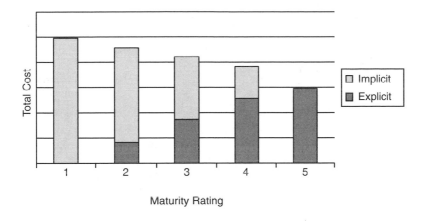

Figure 7.2 Project Performance Costs

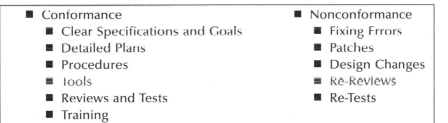

- Conformance
  - Clear Specifications and Goals
  - Detailed Plans
  - Procedures
  - Tools
  - Reviews and Tests
  - Training
- Nonconformance
  - Fixing Errors
  - Patches
  - Design Changes
  - Re-Reviews
  - Re-Tests

Figure 7.3 Cost of Quality in Projects

than the explicit cost of establishing a PMO for the purpose of improving project performance (Figure 7.2). This cost/performance relationship is a variation of the relationship that has already been verified for ensuring quality and the cost of nonconformance to quality standards (Figure 7.3).

The goals of a PMO vary in urgency and sophistication. They include: to set industry standards; to show higher corporate profits; to integrate project management into the organization so that a project management mindset then permeates the organization; to demonstrate that project management is an asset to the enterprise; to improve divisional project management performance; to instill recognition of the project management discipline; to have competent and productive project teams; to implement consistent, formalized project management; or simply to finish a specific project on time and within budget (Figures 7.4 and 7.5). Different types of PMOs solve different types of problems. Therefore, determining organizational objectives that are to be pursued as part of the PMO implementation and functions to be performed by the PMO is the first step in planning the implementation. The amount of funding and the level

Set Industry Standards

Show Higher Corporate Profits

Integrate Project Management into the Organization

Improve Divisional Project Management Performance

Have Competent and Productive Project Teams

Implement Consistent, Formalized Project Management

Finish This Project on Time/within Budget

Figure 7.4   Goals

of corporate commitment are closely linked to these objectives. As noted by Murphy (1997), the principal charter of the PMO is to "help manage the future, not just recalculate the past." The PMO serves to facilitate meaningful change in the organization, not through software tools and techniques but through people who are committed and able to perform new and expanded roles in a new business environment.

When implementing a PMO, attention must be focused on the portions of the strategic direction of the organization that deal with the project management function. One would hope that organizational long-range plans would include such items as reduction of project overruns, improving resource allocation procedures, improving project selection and prioritization, and increasing the delivery speed and enhancing the overall quality of projects. The sophistication of the PMO structure and its funding vary

- ■ Desire for Excellence
- ■ Integration, Consistency
- ■ Quantified Values from
    - ■ Competency of Project Managers
    - ■ Maturity Assessment
        - ■ Internal or External
        - ■ Casual or Detailed
        - ■ For a Division or for the Entire Enterprise
    - ■ Project Evaluation
        - ■ Individual Project or Several Projects
        - ■ Client Success Indicators or Team Success Factors

Figure 7.5   Motivations for Improvement

Goal	Current	Desired
■ Project Specific		
■ Ratings	√	√
■ Overruns	√	√
■ Division Specific		
■ Rating of the Division	√	√
■ Average Ratings of the Projects	√	√
■ Financial Losses Due to Project Failure	√	√
■ Enterprise		
■ Rating of the Organization	√	√
■ Average Rating of the Projects	√	√
■ Financial Losses Due to Project Failure	√	√

Figure 7.6   Improvement Goals

widely depending on whether the overall goals are to improve project-by-project performance, divisional project performance, organizational project performance, or organizational project management maturity, which is the most enlightened of these goals (Figure 7.6).

If the PMO goals are project specific, the goals can be tied either to performance ratings or to cost and schedule overruns. Division-specific goals would highlight the current maturity rating of the division together with the desired rating. Alternately, the objectives can be stated in terms of average evaluation ratings of projects or in terms of a threshold for financial losses due to project failure.

Hopefully, the goals of the PMO are enterprise oriented. The PMO can then institutionalize best practices that it identifies within the organization as it builds a process for project management governance. In this case, the PMO goals become the organizational values of maturity rating, average rating of all the projects, and financial losses that are due to project failure.

The efforts to quantify organizational goals can be focused toward setting organizational standards of performance for each of the project management facets such as cost, schedule, performance, etc. For example, the objectives might state that more than 95% of projects must come in on time, or more than 90% of projects must come in under budget, or that there must be 97% customer satisfaction as a result of project delivery. Therefore, it is necessary to ascertain a realistic picture of the current organizational status. With that information in hand, the design of the PMO can address these specific needs more deliberately.

An alternate method of setting project performance outcomes is to establish quantified standards for a successful project. Then, for each facet, one must specify the performance level that will be considered acceptable. For example, it might be specified that the cost performance

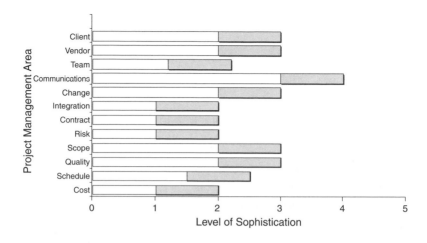

Figure 7.7 Improvement Objectives: Equal Advancement

be rated as perfect if there is a more than 10% under-run. The cost performance is rated as unacceptable if there is a more than 250% overrun. To extend this concept further, one would determine how many of the current projects map unto this range of acceptability, and how many should map unto this range once the PMO is installed. Finally, the improvement objectives could be such that the performance in all areas should be improved by one maturity level, or alternately it could be such that they should all reach a certain level, say, level four (Figures 7.7, 7.8, and 7.9).

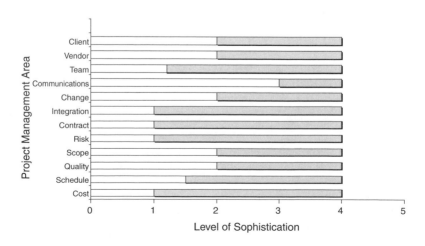

Figure 7.8 Improvement Objectives: Collective Uniform Target

	Objective	Current	Desired
Scope	√	√	
Cost	√	√	
Quality	√	√	
Schedule	√	√	√
Risk	√	√	
Contract	√	√	
Integration	√	√	
Change	√	√	√
Communications	√	√	
Team Relations	√	√	
Client Relations	√	√	
Vendor Relations		√	√

Figure 7.9   Example of Objectives Matrix

7.3 COSTS, BENEFITS

Bernstein (2000) notes that often the suggestion of the implementation of a PMO is met with skepticism as it is equated with increased costs and bureaucracy for the organization. She explains that this view is unfortunate, since the PMO should be considered an ally to the organization and should be viewed as a dynamic addition to the project management process. Her results highlight the fact that a business case must be made for the PMO. The business case must clearly define the benefits that are to be derived from the deliverable of the project. The business case further extends the data to show that the cost of the PMO is justified by the revenues that it would bring to the enterprise. The benefits of the PMO are to attain formalized and consistent project management throughout the organization and to realize improvements in project performance in the areas of cost, schedule, scope, and people. Additional benefits are recognition of the project management discipline and improvement in organizational profitability. It can enable the organization to realize a competitive advantage through reduced project costs.

Englund and Graham (2001) suggest a different approach to determine the value of the PMO to the organization. They recommend that the value be stated in business terms, such as the return on investment of the project office, so that it will be better understood by senior managers. For example, one can determine the increase in shareholder value that would result if a stated goal is reached. This can be done by calculating the benefits if the project-cycle time had been reduced 20% in the past and how this would have increased value on the last five projects that were completed.

Then, the number of projects to be done each year should be estimated along with an estimate of future value of reducing cycle time. It also is necessary to determine how much it will cost to implement the project office. From these figures, then the return on investment of the project office can be estimated.

These benefits can be weighed against the costs of establishing a PMO. These costs include the cost of a permanent staff for enterprise planning, project governance, and customized record keeping; the cost of an appropriate infrastructure for this new organizational entity; and the cost of project management training activities for the organization. Additional costs of establishing a PMO are the costs involved in mentoring, consulting, and augmenting. It is an important point that the intensity and cost of the latter group of activities should diminish as the organization becomes increasingly mature in project management. In fact, the trend in expenditures of time and effort spent in such short-term crisis activities should be a measure of how much the organization has moved toward excellence in project management.

The cost of augmenting, consulting, and mentoring depend on the size of project management staff, and therefore, can be considered remedial operational costs, and not necessarily startup costs. For example, Boehm (1981) in the COCOMO (Constructive Cost Model) cost estimating model notes that the cost of the project office when it is concerned primarily with costs associated with one project represents 4% of the total cost of the project. He classifies functions of the project office as project level management, project planning, contracts, liaison, and status monitoring.

Kwak and Dai (2000) point out that research concerning the contribution of a PMO to overall effectiveness of project management is limited and anecdotal. The Gartner Group (2000, p. 21) found that information systems "organizations that establish enterprise standards for project management, including a project office with suitable governance, will experience half the major project cost overruns, delays and cancellations of those that fail to do so (0.7 probability)."

7.4 ASSESSING THE ORGANIZATION'S CURRENT PROJECT MANAGEMENT PRACTICES

As part of planning for the PMO, one would need to determine, in realistic terms, the status of the organizational environment. To characterize the organizational attitude toward change, one would need to determine if the culture is project oriented or specialty driven. This can be done by assessing the status of the project management practice in the organization. It is necessary to determine how projects are being selected and managed, and the specific methodologies that are being used. To that end, a detailed review of the corporate vision, strategies, and goals must be conducted. Top management must be interviewed in order to highlight the current corporate and business functions of the divisions and personnel within those divisions. Finally, current corporate needs must be detailed to determine the extent of tolerance for inaccurate project data and for project overruns. With this information, the PMO functions that best serve these purposes should be identified. Beyond that, knowledge areas that are most important should be identified. The premise is that operation of the PMO should match the company's strategic project management needs, and that the roles of the PMO in an organization should be methodically defined. It is important not to attempt an overly ambitious implementation in a short period of time.

One approach to determine the most effective PMO for the organization would be to provide answers to the following questions.

7.4.1 Project or Program PMO

A PMO supporting a single project or a group of related projects is recommended if the majority of answers to the following questions are "no," "don't know," or "does not apply."

- Does the project have a project plan that is reviewed and approved by stakeholders inside the organization and by customers?
- Are deliverables and project performance reviewed at the end of each phase of the project?
- Are variances from the project plan in terms of schedule, cost, and performance analyzed and tracked?
- Are changes identified, analyzed, tracked, and managed?
- Does the project have an approved charter that provides authority and responsibility to the project manager and states the project's objectives, scope, assumptions, and constraints?
- Has a WBS been prepared for the project and is it approved before project execution begins?
- Does each project have a work authorization system?
- Are baselines established to monitor performance?
- Has a project schedule been prepared and issued?
- Are cost estimates prepared prior to establishing a project budget?
- Has a forecast of the project's cash flow requirements been prepared?
- Is rework monitored?
- Are roles and responsibilities identified at the work package level of the WBS?
- Is someone available to assist and advise project teams on project management activities?

- Is training available on project management for project professionals throughout the organization?
- Are project team members involved in planning work and in making commitments?
- Are communication requirements identified and planned?
- Are project status reports routinely prepared?
- Are regular project reviews held?
- Are performance deviations from plans identified and analyzed?
- Are issues and action items identified and tracked?
- Are project records maintained in an organized way and archived for use on future projects?
- Are project risks identified, analyzed, tracked, and monitored?
- Is an overall risk ranking for each project prepared?
- Are contingency plans prepared should an identified risk occur?
- Was a project kickoff meeting held?
- Does the project management team participate actively in the source selection and contract administration process?

7.4.2 Division-Level PMO

If the answers to at least 75% of the preceding questions are "yes," then a division-level PMO is appropriate. Next, assess the status of the project management practice in terms of the following questions. If the answers to the majority of these questions are "no," "don't know," or "does not apply," then a division-level PMO is recommended. This PMO will establish standards and methodologies to follow in project management, will review and audit projects that are under way, and will provide mentoring support to project professionals.

- Are reviews conducted to determine whether the project plans comply with organizational procedures?
- Are data evaluated to assess the completeness of project plans?
- Are templates and forms available to assist in the development of project plans? Are these templates reviewed periodically to determine needed enhancements?
- Is a documented procedure followed for managing projects?
- Is information on work results, outcomes of activities performed to accomplish the project, collected and used to assess performance?
- Is oversight of multiple, related projects coordinated?
- Are procedures for integrated change control available and followed?
- Is documentation prepared to show that the customer or sponsor has accepted the product or project phase?
- Are tools and techniques used on projects reviewed periodically?

- Are independent reviews conducted of project cost estimates for comprehensiveness and completeness based on the size, complexity, and significance of the project?
- Are standard metrics collected and analyzed to assess performance on projects?
- Is a quality policy available for the organization and for use on projects?
- Are project audits conducted and is corrective action performed as a result of action items from these audits?
- Is a procedure in place to assign staff to projects?
- Are qualifications and criteria established to recruit and assign project managers?
- Are communications technology factors assessed?
- Is a procedure followed to collect, categorize, disseminate, and archive various types of project information?
- Is a final project review conducted?
- Are checklists available for use in risk identification?
- Are risk-oriented issues conducted with project stakeholders?
- Are risks and risk interdependencies analyzed to assess the range of possible project outcomes?
- Is management involved in determining specific opportunities to pursue and threats to avoid as an outcome of risk identification and analysis?
- Are periodic project risk reviews held?
- Are risk audits conducted?
- Are procurement audits conducted?

7.4.3 Enterprise-Level PMO

If the answers to the majority of the following questions are affirmative, an enterprise-level PMO is most appropriate:

- Is overall customer satisfaction with project deliverables assessed at the end of each project?
- Is a project selection and prioritization process in place?
- Are reviews held periodically to assess the effectiveness of project management procedures used throughout the organization?
- Is a repository of best practice techniques maintained and available for access by project professionals?
- Are projects selected and managed as a portfolio supporting business strategic objectives?
- Are quantitative objectives defined to improve performance in project management?

- Is information collected on the costs and benefits of project work to the organization?
- Are resource utilization and productivity factors available for resource planning on projects?
- Is information collected to assess the overall quality of each project?
- Does the organization have a knowledge management system?
- Are causes of nonconformance identified and classified?
- Does the organization have a project management career path?
- Does the organization have a certification program for its project professionals?
- Are proficiency charts used in conjunction with a competency model to determine the appropriate competency level for each project professional?
- Is a mentoring program available for individuals and for project teams, and are mentoring activities coordinated in the organization?
- Has each project professional prepared an individual development and improvement plan?
- Does each person participate in an organizational project management improvement program?
- Is a team-based reward and recognition system in place?
- Are project team development activities planned and budgeted?
- Is resource use coordinated by the PMO through the integrated management of projects?
- Are resource allocations and individual efforts of project professionals tracked?
- When a new project begins, is it reviewed to determine whether a scaled version of the enterprise's project management methodology should be followed?
- Is a project management information system in use that supports scope, schedule, costs, resource planning and allocation, risks, and change management? Does it interface with the organization's accounting, financial, and human resource systems?
- Can this system be customized for use on projects as appropriate?
- Can stakeholders access the system directly?
- Is the system reviewed periodically to assess its effectiveness?
- Are partnering relationships established with project stakeholders?
- Does the organization have a project management improvement program with quantitative objectives that addresses resources required and workforce training needs?
- Is this project management improvement program reviewed periodically?
- Is external benchmarking conducted to provide a standard for measuring performance?
- Is the PMO function reviewed periodically to assess its effectiveness?

7.5 ASSESSING THE PROJECT-FRIENDLY FEATURE OF THE ORGANIZATIONAL STRUCTURE

Strategy, as described by Alfred Chandler (1962), is "The determination of the basic long-term goals and objectives of an enterprise, and the adoption of courses of action and allocation of resources necessary for carrying out these goals" (p. 13). Chandler's work on the design of modern organizations in pioneering companies led to the conclusion that for organizational structure to be effective and sound, it must follow the organization's strategy. Strategy determines the purpose of structure by clearly defining the vision of the organization, its mission, and its business.

In project management, a spectrum of organizational structures can be adapted based on the specific organizational strategies. In the *PMBOK® Guide* (2000a), Project Management Institute describes these structures as ranging on a continuum from functional to projectized organizations. For each of these structures, characteristics such as the authority of the project manager, the percentage of time that personnel are assigned to project work, the role of the project manager, the titles used for the project manager, and the administrative staff available for project management work are delineated. An extension of this concept will include a description of the role of the PMO.

7.5.1 Functional Organizations

In a functional organization, specialists, or subject matter experts, are grouped together in a single organization unit. Projects that are under way are limited to a specific specialty area and tend not to cross the divisional lines. Project managers typically lack formal authority and rely upon informal relationships to achieve project objectives. Even if administrative support is available, staff tends to support the project manager only on a part-time basis. In these organizations, the project manager serves as an assistant to an executive in the functional unit. The project team is composed of the staff in the functional unit, who works on the project only part time.

In a functional organization, a PMO can be established at the functional unit level to provide staff to support project managers, providing project-focused functions as described previously. However, if it becomes apparent that project work is constituting more and more of the overall work of the organization, then the PMO can begin to provide enterprise-oriented functions for all organizational units.

7.5.2 Project-Oriented Organizations

At the opposite end of the spectrum is the project-oriented organization in which all team members who are required for each project support the project manager on a full-time basis. The project manager has total responsibility for the project. Most of the staff in the organization are involved in project work. As a result, each project has the staff available to handle the project-focused functions described earlier in this book. Thus, the occasions of assistance by the PMO in the areas of augmenting, mentoring, and consulting will be minimized. Therefore, the vast majority of the PMO's effort will be spent on training, archiving, disseminating best practices, and advocating the project management profession.

In a project-oriented structure, the PMO supports the entire organization with a focus on the enterprise-oriented functions. It promotes coordinated efforts in the areas of project selection, prioritization, resource planning, resource allocation, processes, standards, methods, knowledge management, and professional development. The PMO oversees and coordinates the efforts of the individual project office staff that supports each project manager.

7.5.3 Matrix Organizations

The matrix organization consists of characteristics of both the functional and projectized structures. Matrix organizations range from a weak matrix to a strong matrix based on the level of the authority, influence, and power of the project manager, as compared to that of the functional managers. Sometimes titles such as project expediter, project coordinator, or project facilitator signify limited powers. Other indicators of the type of the matrix are: administrative staff that is available to support the project manager, and the amount of time spent on the project by each team member. As noted by Cable and Adams (1989), "the establishment of a project office characterizes the start of the strong matrix" (p. 25). Here, the PMO would provide project-focused functions, and would begin to establish the foundation for enterprise-oriented functions.

7.6 PROJECTS WITH VIRTUAL TEAMS

Increasingly, organizations are using virtual teams to complete projects. Unlike a conventional team, a virtual team works across space, time, and organizational boundaries with links strengthened by webs of communication technologies (Lipnack and Stamps, 1997). Since the virtual project team crosses organizational boundaries, people can be selected who are best suited for the project regardless of their geographic location or organizational unit. Thus, a team response can be implemented virtually and at a reasonable cost, where a co-located team might be too expensive. Additional team members and outside consultants can be added to the project easily without the need for travel costs.

However, there are many challenges and complexities when working in such an environment. Research conducted by Haywood (1998) showed that virtual teams were more difficult to manage and that the key challenge facing virtual project managers was communications difficulties. She found that virtual projects might take longer to complete than conventional projects.

Since the virtual team is dispersed across greater distances, team members cannot communicate easily, at least not using conventional media. Informal communications that occur each day on a co-located team are not available to a virtual team. And, if the team member's functional manager is located on site and is easily accessible, it is often difficult for that virtual team member to focus on the work of the project. In other words, local work may take precedence over project work. It is easy for a team member to feel disengaged from the virtual project and to view it as only something to do after the "real" on-site work is completed. Success of a virtual team depends on clear guidance, constant support, and opportunities to share information. Technologies, policies, and processes are required to facilitate communication, workflow planning and management, relationship building, and knowledge management.

A PMO can be instrumental for successful management of these virtual projects. Since team members may never meet face to face on these projects, a principal focus of the PMO on a virtual project is on information technology and communications. Since continuous anytime communication is required to keep team members connected, the PMO can help establish a communications strategy for the virtual project. Asynchronous chat sessions and electronic document transmission will be used rather than face-to-face discussions and paper exchange.

A global information repository is needed for a virtual project. The PMO can establish and maintain an electronic-based war room or team room for the virtual project. To increase familiarity among the team members, the PMO can include a personal Web page for each team member that includes information about the team member's specific availability and his or her access to useful and interesting tools. An organization chart can be included in the site layout, together with a project team directory. PMO staff can capture project information, store the data in this electronic team room, and make it accessible to all team members at any time. This electronic team room then can provide meeting records, discussion forums, and a repository for project documents, which can link to the organization's knowledge management system. Project management literature can also be made available here.

The virtual team cannot exist effectively without an information technology infrastructure. Therefore, efficiency and reliability of the systems used in project communications and in the project team room are of paramount importance in these projects. If compatible tools are not currently available for each team member's use, then a common data interchange format must be established.

The PMO can provide assistance to project managers in selecting the appropriate information technology products, providing training in their use, and maintaining them in order to empower work collaboration. As new team members join the project, PMO staff can train them in the tools and protocols to be used. At times, an anonymous environment for communication may be required. At other times, it is necessary for everyone to communicate directly, especially when working to generate common understandings of the project. Yet at other times, only a small group of team members may need to communicate on specific technical issues. Therefore, training is required, both in the use of the tools and in methods to communicate, without face-to-face interaction, with specific team members or the entire team. Standards must be established for facilitating agreements between the team members as to when and how they will be available for real-time collaboration, and how they will respond to requests. A system of regular and structured communications through conference calls, online discussion forums, and video conferencing must be established. Every effort should be made to ensure that the technology used is viewed as a method for collaboration rather than as a source of conflict.

On a virtual project, commitment to the project by the project manager and the team members must be stronger than on conventional projects. The PMO in this environment can facilitate development of a team process to define how the team's work will be managed; how workflow will be structured so that all project duties (Figure 7.10) are not consolidated in the same location; how information will be stored, accessed, and shared; and who will review documents and deliverables. It can facilitate the establishment of clear project goals and business outcomes as an under-

```
■ Planning
■ Conceptual Design
■ Testing
■ Detailed Design
■ Product Evaluation
■ Project Management
■ Centralized System Administration
■ Local System Management
■ Help Desk
■ Online Support
```

Figure 7.10 Project Duties (Virtual or Traditional)

lying foundation for the virtual team's work. The PMO can establish a procedure to rotate administrative tasks among team members on a regular basis. Such sharing of duties can help make a virtual team seem more tangible to its members.

Geographical dispersion can have cultural implications in communications. Language barriers and time differences present other challenges. For example, information may be interpreted differently because of a cultural misperception. An idea, behavior, or attitude expressed by the team member may be the result of a different cultural value. The PMO can help minimize any misunderstandings that may be due to cultural differences of the virtual project team. Finally, the PMO staff can work with individual team members of a virtual project if it appears that a team member may feel out of the loop, or if it is evident that a team member is not fully participating.

Because of the lack of collocation with the project manager, each team member will need more assurances that his or her contributions are valued, and that his or her ideas will be heard, and that such ideas will be developed to the benefit of the project. Each team member must feel that he or she has visibility to the project manager and to the upper management. More than collocated teams, and probably in different forms, virtual teams require work protocols including how to resolve conflicts, how to escalate issues, how to ensure each person is participating, and how to handle administrative activities. Finally, performance and productivity information must be shared. As stated by Lipnack and Stamps (1997), "An individual without information cannot take responsibility; an individual who is given information cannot help but take responsibility."

7.7 PMO IMPLEMENTATION PROJECT

Implementation of PMO must be treated just like any other project, more so just to highlight effective planning and execution. It is important to identify the success criteria for the PMO and for project management in the organization. Metrics must be established to measure the improvements as a result of the implementation of the PMO. In tangible terms, possible impacts of the PMO on the following must be identified: individual projects, project portfolio, project cost impact, morale improvement, and operational benefits. A top-down implementation is recommended so that the PMO is not viewed as another layer of bureaucracy but rather as an organizational unit that adds value to the enterprise.

First, the PMO must be set up and established as an entity in the organization. As such, it must be properly staffed, and ample office space must be available. A charter for PMO implementation is needed, similar to a charter for a specific project. Here, the charter will specify the purpose of the PMO in the organization. The charter will provide the PMO with the authority and responsibility to apply organizational resources to the activities that are within the PMO's purview. The sponsor of the PMO should prepare the charter and sign off on it. He or she also should obtain concurrence and sign-offs by appropriate executive managers throughout the organization. This charter will highlight executive support for PMO implementation, and it serves as the springboard for the PMO's subsequent activities (see Appendix 7A). The PMO organization chart, including roles and responsibilities, must be prepared and disseminated to the organization.

Next, the PMO must prepare a detailed plan for its operations. The plan should contain specific objectives of the organization as they support the vision for project management activities (Figure 7.11). To that end, the plan must specify milestones, such as first visible impact, intermediate milestones, and completion target (Figures 7.12 and 7.13). The PMO requires a scope statement, a WBS (Figure 7.14), metrics to measure its performance, and a communications management plan. And, like any other project, the plan for the PMO implementation must be distributed to the stakeholders for information, review, comment, and approval (Figure 7.15). The PMO implementation plan must be comprehensive and include a statement of objectives, network diagram, bar chart, tabular information, total cost estimate, roles and responsibilities, and necessary cash flow (Figures 7.16 and 7.17). Communication management approaches must be described. During regular reporting cycles, appropriate progress reports must be issued indicating the variances and plan modifications

- Determine Project Success
  - Client Success Indicators
  - Team Success Factors
- Assess Project Management Maturity
  - Division
  - Enterprise
- Quantify Project Manager Competency
  - Project Performance
  - Credentials
  - Continuing Education
- Quantify Project Team Competency
  - Team Member Performance Indicators
  - Task Performance Indicators

Figure 7.11   Indices of Performance: Project Success Attributes

■ Metrics for Success Evaluation
■ Intermediate Milestones and Metrics
  ■ First noticeable improvement
  ■ Intermediate benefits
  ■ Short term, 3 months
    ■ Overall organizational impact
    ■ Immediate methodology needs
  ■ Mid term, 3–6 months
    ■ Roll out operational PMO
    ■ Support function
  ■ Long term, beyond 6 months
    ■ Fully functional PMO
    ■ Implement project portfolio database
    ■ Formalize report generation and distribution

Figure 7.12　Develop Implementation Milestones

■ Project
  ■ 3 Months–1 Year
■ Division
  ■ 1–3 Years
■ Enterprise
  ■ 3–7 Years

Figure 7.13　Schedule Rule of Thumb

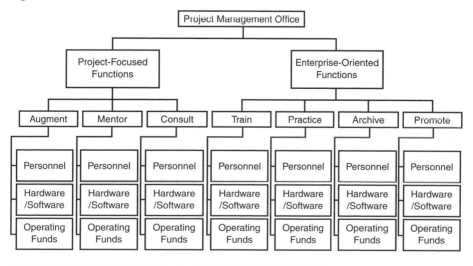

Figure 7.14　WBS for PMO

> - Develop Organization-Specific PM Procedures
>   - In All Areas of Project Management
>   - For All Divisions
> - Use as Basis for
>   - Promoting
>   - Training
>   - Consulting
>   - Mentoring
>   - Augmenting
>   - Disseminating
>   - Archiving

Figure 7.15   PMO Implementation Plan

> - Personnel
>   - All PMO Functional Areas
>   - Promote, Train, Consult, Mentor, Augment, Practice, Archive
> - Infrastructure
>   - Support Staff
>   - Physical Plant
>   - Funding for Professional Activities to Maintain Currency

Figure 7.16   PMO Cost

	Cost of the Infrastructure to						
	Promote	Archive	Practice	Train	Consult	Mentor	Augment
Scope	√	√	√	√	√	√	√
Cost	√	√	√	√	√	√	√
Quality	√	√	√	√	√	√	√
Schedule	√	√	√	√	√	√	√
Risk	√	√	√	√	√	√	√
Contract	√	√	√	√	√	√	√
Integration	√	√	√	√	√	√	√
Reporting	√	√	√	√	√	√	√
Communications	√	√	√	√	√	√	√
Team Relations	√	√	√	√	√	√	√
Client Relations	√	√	√	√	√	√	√
Vendor Relations	√	√	√	√	√	√	√

Figure 7.17   Estimate the Effort

- Shortfall in
  - People Issues Management
  - Things Issues Management
- Span of PMO Activities
  - Core Organization
  - Operations at the Steady-State Level
  - Recovery Activities
  - Preventative Activities
- Span of Influence
  - Project
  - Division
  - Organization

Figure 7.18 Schedule/Cost Factors

At this point, the PMO staff members would be cognizant of the scope of their responsibilities and the manner in which they are to interact with others in the organization. The implementation of the PMO represents a major cultural change for the organization. Therefore, time must be set aside for meetings with stakeholders to discuss the added value that the PMO staff brings to the organization. A number of briefings and even workshops may be required so that people throughout the organization recognize the purpose of the PMO (Figure 7.18). The PMO must be viewed as a complementary and supportive unit, and not as a rigid administrative structure that does not allow the necessary creativity and flexibility that project managers require.

Successful implementation depends on the staff assigned to the PMO. The staff needs knowledge of the current business processes in the organization and experience in dealing with the current model of operation. Competency in project management is measured by project performance, credentials, or formal training.

The life-cycle phases for the PMO implementation project should consist of the following five steps (Figure 7.19).

- Establish Vision and Strategy
- Prepare the Execution Plan
- Establish Priorities
- Assist Individual Projects
- Operate and Maintain the PMO

Figure 7.19 PMO Life Cycle

1. ***Establish the vision and strategy.*** The PMO can be an add-on to the existing method of project management in the organization, the PMO can be established to implement new and revised business activities for project management in the organization, or the PMO can be established to manage all project management functions in the organization. Therefore, the vision for the PMO should be flexible. One must consider issues such as how would the organization change because of the PMO, what is the direction of the organization in terms of project management, and what is included and excluded in project management. To define the PMO strategy, one must consider what the organization is doing now in project management, and then identify current assumptions and constraints. One must also assess the organizational key factors for success, competitors' programs and priorities, the organization's strengths and weaknesses in light of the competition, and likely external changes. Based on the information thus collected, one must define what PMO alternative would best suit the organizational direction.

2. ***Prepare a plan for the PMO program to guide its execution.*** This plan should include a transition plan for the PMO. Changes in culture, power, and responsibilities will be required. The plan should guide the implementation of the PMO, eliminate or reduce uncertainty in roles and responsibilities, document assumptions and constraints, provide a basis for monitoring and controlling the PMO implementation, and facilitate communication with stakeholders. The plan should include organizational interfaces because barriers between organizations need to be eliminated to facilitate knowledge management. A steering group composed of representatives from the various organizational units should be involved in the preparation of this plan. The steering group must review and sign off on it to foster commitment and buy in.

3. ***Plan and establish priorities.*** The PMO's initial focus should be on the largest problems that are blocking improved project results. It may be necessary to concentrate on mentoring and augmenting functions if the PMO concept is just being introduced throughout the organization. Over time, the emphasis will change to focus more on training and promoting functions in order to effectively champion project management culture throughout the organization.

4. ***Facilitate collaborative work.*** Since project management processes and practices will need to be modified, staff from all stakeholder organizations should actively participate during the implementation. The nature of the PMO is such that it requires collaborative work. Greater involvement can foster greater commitment, increased sharing of lessons learned, improved coordination, and early warning about problems.

5. ***Assist and facilitate the organization's projects.*** At this point, the PMO will shepherd individual projects. To that end, the PMO will implement consistent methodologies for managing cost, schedule, scope, and quality of a few projects. It is recommended that such conversions be conducted on pilot projects before full implementation on larger projects. Further, if the organization is just beginning to move into project management, a pilot approach of using a PMO to assist one program, division, or organizational unit is recommended. Finally, not all functions can be implemented at once, and not everywhere at once, either.

6. ***Operate and maintain the PMO.*** Once the PMO is operational, its activities must be tracked and monitored by collecting and analyzing metrics. Periodically, an external audit should be conducted of the efforts under way. Such audits will consider the perspectives of the PMO staff, project managers in the organization, functional managers, and executive management. Since executive management provides the vision, resources, and policies to resolve issues, their involvement should be continuous, but noninterfering. The executive management is expected to conduct reviews of the PMO's effectiveness in the light of continuous improvement initiatives. The executive management then communicates the results and progress to all the stakeholders.

A staged implementation plan is recommended for the PMO, primarily because such implementation is a long-term project. The overall concept is simple and logical, but it involves many elements and steps.

7.8 DEPLOYMENT OF THE PMO

Factors that influence support for a PMO stem from organizational objectives for excellence and from the level of organizational support. The organizational desire for excellence can be focused at project-by-project performance, divisional project success, organizational project management performance, or an objective to achieve a specific organizational project management maturity level. The issues that define organizational support in establishment of the PMO are the level of funding allocated to the PMO, the possibility of disturbing the status quo, and the likelihood of triggering changes in the balance of power in the organizational structure.

As for deployment of the PMO, the higher the goals, the higher should be the placement of the PMO (Figure 7.20). As a first approximation, the region of influence of PMO will extend to all the organizational units that report to the PMO's sponsor. If the PMO is a unit of a single project, the benefits of the PMO can only be felt within the project (Figure 7.21). On the other hand, if the PMO reports to the CEO of the company, then the

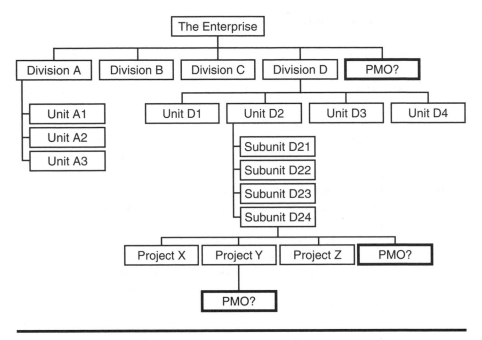

Figure 7.20 PMO Placement

policies, procedures, and enhancements effected by PMO will have profound effects on all aspects of organizational endeavor (Figure 7.22). One must assess the current situation in the organization to determine the status of organizational practices and the work that must be done and then design a PMO that will best support the organization considering the ongoing practices, competencies, goals, resistance to change, politics, values, and preferences (Figure 7.23). The important point is that the PMO serve the organization's needs. A staged approach may be required, starting first with the PMO supporting a project or series of projects and then supporting cross-functional projects, and finally supporting all projects in the organization with a full range of functions. However, greater benefits will accrue if the PMO is placed at the highest operational level possible, as this will demonstrate sustained executive sponsorship.

Ideally, the PMO should be equipped for all of the elements of its charter. With proper implementation and operation of the PMO, one hopes that two significant observations will be made over time. First, the overall effort necessary by the PMO to assist and facilitate the project activities should decrease with time. The other significant observation should be in the mixture of the functions. As the organization matures, a smaller portion of the PMO's effort will be spent on augmenting, mentoring, and consulting, thus signaling that the crisis management mode of project management is no longer practiced in this organization (Figure 7.24).

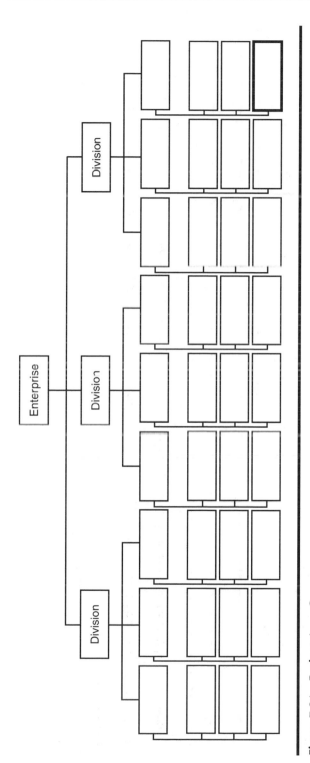

Figure 7.21   Project Area Coverage

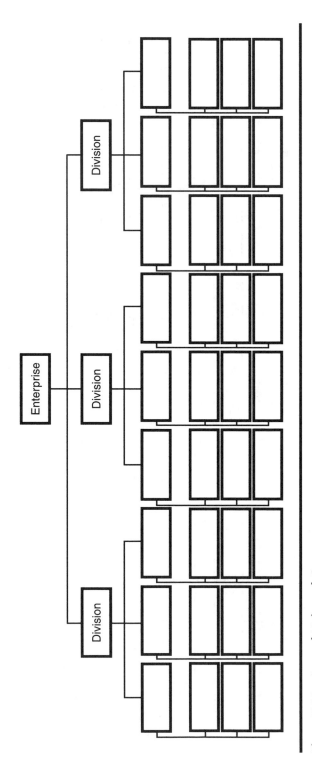

Figure 7.22 Area of Universal Coverage

	Project	Division	Organization
Promote	√	√	√
Archive	√	√	√
Practice	√	√	√
Train	√	√	√
Consult	√	√	√
Mentor	√	√	√
Augment	√	√	√

Figure 7.23   Estimate the Number of Beneficiaries and Organizational Coverage

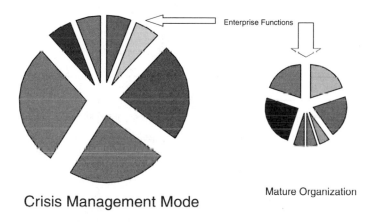

Crisis Management Mode

Mature Organization

Figure 7.24   PMO Activities

CONCLUSIONS

Implementation of the PMO should be planned and executed just like any other project. As such, attention should be paid to the project objectives in terms of administrative placement, schedule, cost, and metrics by which the outcome of the project is measured. Once the PMO has been fully operational for a while, not only will the organizational burden of failed projects lighten, but at the same time, the overall operational cost of the PMO should also decrease.

APPENDIX 7A
PROJECT MANAGEMENT
OFFICE CHARTER

Director, PMO	Phone	Fax	E mail
VP of Projects	Phone	Fax	E-mail
Objectives			
Scope			
Responsibilities			
Assumptions			
Constraints			
Major Risks			
Major Milestones			
Approvals:			
Director, PMO	Signature		Date
VP of Projects	Signature		Date
Vice President #1	Signature		Date
Vice President #2	Signature		Date
Vice President #N	Signature		Date

8

THE PMO AND PROFESSIONAL RESPONSIBILITY

8.1 OVERVIEW

Each project consists of a series of decisions of varying degrees of importance. These decisions force us to choose how best to respond, behave, or react. In many situations, we must make trade-offs, in terms of schedule, cost, and quality considerations. Personal, technical, and organizational influences must be considered. Customer satisfaction is also a significant concern. On projects, often it is difficult to even know who the customer is, and yet the project manager must manage competing interests among multiple customers. Many items affect each project decision. As noted by Project Management Institute in the *PMBOK® Guide* (2000a), project decisions extend beyond the organization and include social, economic, and environmental influences. With the increasing globalization of project management, project activities have assumed greater dimensions. Accordingly, "organizations are increasingly accountable for impacts resulting from a project... as well as for the effects of a project on people, the economy, and the environment long after it has been completed" (p. 27).

Therefore, each person working on a project must take responsibility for his or her actions. The importance of this facet of duties was noted by Project Management Institute in its *Project Management Professional (PMP) Role Delineation Study* (2000b). Here, Project Management Institute held a series of meetings to define the responsibilities of professionals in project management. The meetings resulted in identification of several performance domains that define the project management profession. These domains consisted of the five process groups in the *PMBOK® Guide*

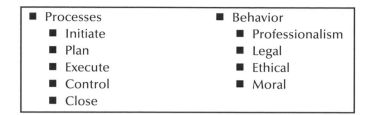

Figure 8.1   Project Manager's Responsibilities

(initiating, planning, executing, controlling, and closing), with the addition of one new domain: professional responsibility. The new domain covers legal, ethical, moral, and professional behavior (Figure 8.1).

Any routine decisions that you make as a project manager or team member will have professional responsibility aspects. Difficult choices may need to be made. Decisions may affect an employee's life, a vendor's ability to stay in business, or a customer's safety. Decision making based on lack of a clear consensus, or based on incomplete information, is a fact of life in project work. Not everything is quantifiable or predictable. It is important to think through the consequences of each decision, often with very little time available in which to do so. Alternatives must be considered. As a project professional, one must decide the right course of action to pursue. One must step back and consider the broader implications of the decisions that are made.

Sometimes, it is difficult to articulate the actual dilemma, and as a result, it then becomes difficult to formulate clear, possible solutions. In project management, this is a special challenge, given the incomplete or ambiguous and ever-changing project requirements, the multiple points of view of the many different stakeholders, and conflicting responsibilities between project managers and their functional manager counterparts. There is no structured methodology that can be followed in every situation. Therefore, much of our project behavior is derived from the personal decisions we make about what we believe is the right thing to do or the wrong thing to do. In other words, considerable judgment is required.

The dilemma is how can we best ensure that we are taking professional responsibility for our actions. There are no universal rules or guidelines to follow. Ultimately, your conscience must always be more important to you than what others, who may not be fully informed about your circumstances, think about you. Further, it is important to be able to structure and record the decisions that are made to be able to explain them to everyone involved.

Professional responsibility as a project manager is tied directly to one's personal sense of responsibility, both to the profession and to one's own organization. As Rosen et al. (2000) notes, people, relationships, and culture are inextricably linked. "The challenge for all of us is to learn how to learn." Project Management Institute (2000b) sets forth five different tasks and knowledge and skill statements within the professional responsibility performance domain that the PMO can use as the starting point for guidance to its project management professionals in this area. But the issue of professional behavior should be interwoven in all five of these areas.

8.2 ENSURING INTEGRITY AND PROFESSIONALISM

Project Management Institute (2000b) states the importance of ensuring integrity and professionalism by adhering to legal requirements and ethical standards. This is done to protect the project management community and all stakeholders. The foundation of this process is the knowledge of legal requirements, ethical standards, community values, and shareholder values. Again, appropriate judgment is required in interpreting the requirements and adapting them to the situation at hand.

Project Management Institute has set forth ethical standards of conduct for its members and a code of conduct for certified Project Management Professionals. The PMO can establish similar standards for project personnel in its organization, with a focus on encouraging actions in an ethical and professional manner. It can state specific responsibilities to customers, users, the public and other stakeholders in light of the organization's vision and specific values. The PMO can outline specific legal requirements and other requirements unique to the organization that must be followed. For example, the PMO can note in these standards how a project professional should best handle a conflict of interest situation. These standards should not be stated in terms of a checklist but rather as guidelines to consider when difficult situations arise. A checklist might discourage considerations as to the implications of each decision. Instead, the emphasis should be placed on how to interpret legal requirements, evaluate decisions, and ensure consistency in one's actions.

Further, the PMO can provide facilitative support to project professionals to help promote individual integrity and professionalism. The facilitative role is particularly important; often it is helpful to have a neutral party to consult to help think through a specific decision. As a facilitator, the PMO staff member can serve as a personal performance advisor to help handle difficult situations. PMO staff members, who have the proper vantage point and experience in project management, will understand what is involved in terms of the challenges of managing each project. Consequently, they can highlight those solutions that they have seen to be effective in similar situations, and those solutions that are not appropriate and should be avoided. In this role, the PMO staff can offer suggestions to consider, including available resources, problem-solving approaches, and opportunities to "think out loud" with the project team member (Flannes and Levin, 2001).

8.3 CONTRIBUTING TO THE PROJECT MANAGEMENT KNOWLEDGE BASE

The importance of contributing to the project management knowledge base has been highlighted by Project Management Institute (2000b). This is done by sharing lessons learned, best practices, and research. As a result, the profession is advanced, and the capabilities of each professional are increased.

One of the major functions of the PMO, at both the project and enterprise levels, is in knowledge management. The PMO's focus is on the development of new knowledge in project management and new uses for existing knowledge. The PMO understands the knowledge of the impact of the project on the business, and on the culture and procedures of the organization. Rather than just collecting data and filing them away, the PMO focus is on collecting lessons learned on projects and then using them to promote positive change within the organization. In other words, the PMO converts these data into useful and reliable information that is accessible by future projects.

So that decisions can be based on knowledge rather than opinion, the PMO establishes a knowledge management system for use by project professionals. Through the PMO's leadership, a community of practice in project management in the organization can be established. The PMO's goal is to promote continuous improvement in the organization's project management practice. This can only be done by a focus on knowledge management, and by using this knowledge as the basis for decisions and actions on projects. It is important to recognize that each decision must be based on sound knowledge.

8.4 ENHANCING INDIVIDUAL COMPETENCE

As part of the professional responsibility domain, Project Management Institute (2000b) stresses the need to enhance individual competence to increase and apply professional knowledge, and to improve services. Proper project performance has a direct relationship on project success, and the competency of the project manager provides the basis for project performance (Project Management Institute, 2001).

Enhancing individual competence is in line with the the PMO's enterprise function of professional development. By establishing competency standards, the PMO can assist project professionals in successful management of their project work. It can establish specific behaviors, knowledge, and abilities required for each project management position. The PMO will then disseminate these descriptions and guidelines to project management professionals throughout the organization. This in turn can lead to the identification of specific training needs and certification requirements that show the knowledge, skills, and abilities required for success at each project management level based on these competency standards. The PMO further establishes job descriptions and a project management career path. At the enterprise level, the PMO can identify future project needs, anticipate job openings, and identify the best candidates for the positions.

8.5 BALANCING STAKEHOLDERS' INTERESTS

The fourth item on the knowledge and skill statement addresses the need to balance stakeholders' interests. In order to satisfy competing needs and objectives, one would need to exercise judgment to determine a fair resolution, negotiate, communicate effectively, and resolve conflicts (Project Management Institute, 2000b).

As projects move more toward a customer-driven approach (Barkley and Saylor, 1995), the PMO can perform a key role in this area. Building and maintaining relationships with customers and stakeholders is a continual process and cannot be taken for granted. Often, projects fail as a result of poor customer relationship management. The PMO can promote, at the enterprise level, a unified vision with a focus on customer understanding and the establishment of long-term customer relationships. It can establish a template for a customer relationship management plan to address items such as formal customer identification, commitment management, communications management, reporting requirements, information distribution, and customer satisfaction management.

Projects tend to serve the needs of multiple customers. In many cases it is difficult to recognize all of the customer's requirements and to satisfy them. The PMO can provide guidelines to help project teams conduct a stakeholder analysis as part of the project management methodology. Because customers may have competing requirements, the PMO can establish a requirements analysis and requirements management process. The PMO can help facilitate requirements gathering sessions among customers through approaches such as surveys, interviews, focus groups, and usability studies. It can provide support in gathering and interpreting requirements, since well-defined requirements will provide the technical baseline for the project. Staying abreast of technological developments in the area, the PMO can also recommend the most recent requirements management tools for use on projects. Once the requirements have been defined, the PMO will work with the customers to ensure that their needs and requirements have been expressed clearly and to establish acceptance criteria for the project. Further, it can assist project teams in establishing a requirements repository for management of changes that will inevitably occur throughout the project life cycle. This process will help ensure that the quality that is expected and envisioned by the client is the same as the actual quality that the project delivers.

To encourage participation in broader decisions about customer requirements and project progress, the PMO can assist team members in looking beyond their own individually assigned work packages and specific project responsibilities. This process can help link the organization's and the project's purposes to customer requirements. The PMO can take a broader view and help facilitate a partnership with customers from beginning to end.

At times, the conflicting requirements among customers and stakeholders may be such that conflicts on the project are rampant. As noted by Meredith and Mantel (2000), conflict in the project world is inevitable since project management involves a number of different stakeholders, including the project team, customers, performing organization, suppliers, and interested parties. If the conflicts are not addressed properly, the conflict can undercut the potential project success. Again, the PMO can serve to facilitate the identification of differences between the project team and the stakeholders and the resolution of these differences. As a facilitator, the PMO will work with the team to discuss appropriate conflict resolution methods to use in different stages of the project. The positive and negative applications of each approach will be highlighted.

Customer retention is a key factor in competitive success and is closely tied to customer satisfaction. As a result, projects are measured in terms of customer satisfaction, and the PMO can periodically assess customer satisfaction through surveys and interviews. For all projects that are under way in the organization, the PMO can establish a system of customer satisfaction measurement. Customer feedback is then used for continuous project management improvement. Then, by examining trends in customer satisfaction indices and by linking satisfaction data to internal processes, the PMO can observe trends and identify areas for improvement.

8.6 RESPECTING PERSONAL, ETHNIC, AND CULTURAL DIFFERENCES

Finally, Project Management Institute (2000b) stresses the importance of interacting with the team and stakeholders in a professional and cooperative manner. This behavioral facet requires respect for personal, ethnic, and cultural differences.

With virtual teams becoming more and more common on projects, the cultural characteristics of project teams become a critical concern of all project professionals. Incongruity between implicit, culture-based assumptions by people of diverse ethnic backgrounds, and corresponding perceptions by others, can cause significant personal clashes. As a result, embracing diversity, exhibiting empathy, exercising tolerance, and advocating compromise become more important.

Culture impacts projects in many ways. Research indicates that one's ethnic culture has a more significant influence on one's way of thinking and acting than the organization's culture. No matter how well a project professional tries to adapt to an organization's culture, he or she will still be driven primarily by his or her latent and innate culture (Minor, 1999). While working with geographically dispersed teams, project professionals must deal with many new challenges: language barriers, time differences, and socioeconomic, political, and religious diversity — and even unfamiliar eating habits! It is important for all project personnel to be sensitive to these cultural differences and to take special care to minimize, and perhaps avoid, the potential risks associated with them.

The PMO can foster the use of computer-mediated communication to maintain a centralized repository of information (such as a dedicated Web site and electronic reference book) on the various cultures, countries, and languages that are represented in both the performing organization and the customer's organizations. This approach can help project participants acquire a keener sensitivity to the various cultural differences among them, as they move into projects with different team members. Further, software that supports multiple languages, and enables interactive translation in individual workstations, can be used to build interpersonal cross-cultural bridges. Creative uses of Web-based e-mail, voice-mail, electronic bulletin boards, and teleconferencing (using both video and audio systems) can also be established to help stimulate, accelerate, and enrich the cross-cultural and transnational projects. The objective is to minimize historical and linguistically embedded barriers so that there are fluid communication flows instead (Sohmen and Levin, 2001).

CONCLUSIONS

Professional responsibility is assuming greater importance in project management. The PMO can assist its project professionals in this area through mentoring and consulting and by providing guidelines. These guidelines will highlight integrity, professionalism, knowledge management, individual competence stakeholder issues, and cultural diversity. Although these guidelines provide tools to help determine behavior in delicate situations, the final decision depends heavily on your personal values, and your own sense of right and wrong.

REFERENCES

Anonymous, A cleanup project can't get going, *High Country News, Western Roundup*, 29(18), September 29, 1997a.

Anonymous, Deep problems at Pit 9, *Bulletin of the Snake River Alliance*, 11(2), Fall 1997b.

Anonymous, *Skills and Knowledge of Cost Engineering*, 4th ed., AACE, Morgantown, WV, September 1999.

Anonymous, Central Artery/Tunnel Project, *Project Management Monthly*, February 28, 2001.

Arter, D.R. *Quality Audits for Improved Performance*, 2nd ed., ASQC Quality Press, Milwaukee, WI, 1994.

Ashley, D.B., Lurie, C.S., and Jaselskis, E.J., Determinants of construction project success, *Project Management Journal*, 18(2), 1987.

Augustine, T. and Schroeder, C., An effective metrics process model, *Crosstalk*, 12(6), 4, June 1999.

Baily, R., Six steps to project recovery, *PM Network*, 14(5), May 2000.

Barkley, B.T. and Saylor, J.H., Customerizing project management, *Project Management Journal*, 8(3), September 1995.

Berg, C. and Colenso, K., WBS practice standard, *PM Network*, 14(4), 69, April 2000.

Bernstein, S., Project offices in practice, *Project Management Journal*, 31(4), 4, December 2000.

Block, T.R., The project office phenomenon, *PM Network*, 12(3), 45, March 1998.

Boehm, B.W., *Software Engineering Economics*, Prentice-Hall, Englewood Cliffs, NJ, 1981.

Bowers, L.J., Demise of the Superconducting Super Collider, *SRA Journal*, 25(4), 51, Spring 1994.

Boyatzis, R.E., *The Competent Manager: A Model for Effective Performance*, John Wiley & Sons, New York, 1982.

Boynton, A.C. and Zmud, R.W., An assessment of critical success factors, *Sloan Management Review*, 26(4), Summer 1984.

Bullen, C.V. and Rockart, J.F., A primer on critical success factors, *Sloan CISR WP*, 69, June 1981.

Byrd, T., *The Making of the Channel Tunnel*, Thomas Telford, London, 1994.

Cable, D. and Adams, J.R., *Organizing for Project Management*, Third Printing, Project Management Institute, Upper Darby, PA, November 1989.

Casey, W. and Peck, W., Choosing the right PMO setup, *PM Network*, 15(2), 48, February 2001.

Chandler, A.D., *Strategy and Structure: Chapters in the History of the Industrial Enterprise*, MIT Press, Cambridge, MA, 1962.

Cleland, D. and Kerzner, H., *A Project Management Dictionary of Terms,* Van Nostrand Reinhold, New York, 1985.

Crawford, L., Assessing and developing project management competence, Proceedings of the 30th Annual Project Management Institute 1999 Seminars & Symposium, Philadelphia, 1999.

Deloitte & Touche, Central Artery/Tunnel Project: Project Assessment, August 3, 2000.

Dinsmore, P.C., Positioning the project management office, *PM Network*, 14(8), 28, August 2000a.

Dinsmore, P.C., Project office, does one size fit all? *PM Network*, 14(4), 28, April 2000b.

Dobbins, J.H. and Donnelly, R.G., Critical success factors in DOD program management, *Acquisition Review Quarterly*, Summer 1998.

Dymond, K.M., *A Guide to the CMM*, Process Inc., Annapolis, MD, 1995.

Englund, R.L. and Graham, R.J., Implementing a project office for organizational change, *PM Network*, 15(2), 48, February 2001.

Fairweather, V., The Channel Tunnel: larger than life, and late, *Civil Engineering*, 64, 42, May 1994.

Fetherston, D., *The Chunnel: The Amazing Story of the Undersea Crossing of the English Channel,* Time-Life Books, New York, 1997.

Flannes, S.W. and Levin, G., *People Skills for Project Managers*, Management Concepts, Vienna, VA, 2001.

Fleming, Q.W. and Koppelman, J.M., Project teams: the role of the project office, *Cost Engineering*, 40(8), 33, August 1998.

Florac, W.A., Park, R.E., and Carleton, A.D., *Practical Software Measurement: Measuring for Process Management and Improvement*, Software Engineering Institute, Pittsburgh, PA, 1997, CMU/SEI-97-HB-003.

Frame, J.D., *Project Management Competence. Building Key Skills for Individuals, Teams, and Organizations*, Jossey-Bass Publishers, San Francisco, 1999.

Frame, J.D. and Block, T.R., *The Project Office*, Crisp Publications, Menlo Park, CA, 1998.

Gadeken, O., Project managers as leaders: competencies of top performers, Proceedings of Internet '94, World Congress of Project Management, Oslo, Norway, 1994.

Gartner Group, The Project Office: Teams, Processes, and Tools, Gartner Research, A Strategic Analysis Report, Analytical Source: Matt Light, August 1, 2000.

Haywood, M., *Managing Virtual Teams: Practical Techniques for High-Technology Project Managers*, Artech House, Boston, 1998.

Hillier, A.M. and McDermott, R.M., The launch of the Channel Tunnel, Project Management Institute Seminar/Symposium, San Francisco, September 17–21, 1988.

Humphrey, W.S., *Managing the Software Process*, Addison-Wesley, Reading, MA, 1989.

Ibbs, W.C. and Kwak, Y., *The Benefits of Project Management*, Project Management Institute Educational Foundation, Newtown Square, PA, 1997.

Kerzner, H., *Applied Project Management*, John Wiley & Sons, New York, 2000.

Kerzner, H., *Strategic Planning for Project Management Using a Project Management Maturity Model*, John Wiley & Sons, New York, 2001.

Kwak, Y.H. and Dai, C.X.Y. Assessing the value of project management offices (PMO), Proceedings of PMI Research Conference 2000, Project Management Institute, Newtown Square, PA, 2000.

Lemley, Jack K., The Channel tunnel: creating a modern wonder-of-the-world, *PM Network*, 7(7), 14, July 1992.

Levin, G., The changing nature of the project audit: no longer a "gotcha game," Proceedings of the 29th Annual Project Management Institute 1998 Seminars & Symposium, Long Beach, CA, 1998.

Levin, G., Metrics for project management maturity, *Project World*, Boston, May 1999.

Levin, G., Hill, G.M., DeFillipis, P., Ward, J.L., and Shaltry, P., *ProjectFRAMEWORK: A Project Management Maturity Model*, ESI International, Arlington, VA, 1999.

Lipnack, J. and Stamps, J., *Virtual Teams: Reaching across Space, Time, and Organizations with Technology*, John Wiley & Sons, New York, 1997.

Lubianinker, S. and Levin, G., Using the Web for next generation project management assessments, Proceedings of the 32nd Annual Project Management Institute 2001 Seminars & Symposium, Nashville, TN, 2001.

Luftman, J., *Competing in the Information Age: Practical Applications of the Strategic Alignment Model*, Oxford University Press, New York, 1996.

Lullen, L.L. and Sylvia, R., Getting organized: implementing the project office, *PM Network*, 13(4), 51, April 1999.

Meredith, J.R. and Mantel, S.J., Jr., *Project Management: A Managerial Approach*, 4th ed., John Wiley & Sons, New York, 2000.

Minor, W.R., Stranger in a strange land: the American project manager working abroad, *PM Network*, 13(3), 31, March 1999.

Murphy, R.E., The role of the project support office, *PM Network*, 11(5), 33, May 1997.

O'Hara, S. and Levin, G., Using metrics to demonstrate the value of project management, Proceedings of the 31st Annual Project Management Institute 2000 Seminars & Symposium, Houston, TX, 2000.

Pearson, A.W., Project selection in an organizational context, *IEEE Transactions on Engineering Management*, 21(4), 152, 1974.

Pinto, J.K. and Prescott, J.E., Variations in critical success factors over the stages in the project lifecycle, *Journal of Management*, 14(1), 1988.

Pinto J.K. and Slevin, D.P., Critical factors in successful project implementation, *IEEE Transaction on Engineering Management*, 34(1), 22, February 1987.

Pinto, J.K. and Slevin, D.P., Critical success factors across the project life cycle, *Project Management Journal*, 19(3), 1988.

Project Management Institute, *The Future of Project Management*, Project Management Institute, Newtown Square, PA, 1999.

Project Management Institute, *A Guide to the Project Management Body of Knowledge. PMBOK® Guide*, 2000 Edition, Project Management Institute, Newtown Square, PA, 2000a.

Project Management Institute, *Project Management Professional (PMP) Role Delineation Study*, Project Management Institute, Newtown Square, PA, 2000b.

Project Management Institute, *Project Manager Competency Development Framework Exposure Draft*, Project Management Institute, Newtown Square, PA, 2001.

Rad, P.F., *Project Estimating and Cost Management*, Management Concepts, Vienna, VA, 2002.

Rad, P.F. and Raghavan, A., Establishing an organizational project office, Proceedings of the Annual Meeting of the Association for Advancement of Cost Engineering, June 2000.

Rockart, J.F., Chief executives define their own data needs, *Harvard Business Review*, 57(2), March 1979.

Rosen, R., Digh, P., Singer, M., and Phillips, C., *Global Literacies Lessons on Business Leadership and National Cultures*, Simon & Schuster, New York, 2000.

Rubin, A.J., Super Collider surges ahead despite concerns over cost, *Congressional Quarterly Weekly Report*, 40(14), 856, April 6, 1991.

Schlichter, J., Surveying project management capabilities, *PM Network*, 13(4), 39, April 1999.

Schwartz, M., Project manager priorities, *Software Magazine*, January 1998, www.softwaremag.com.

Scotto, M., The project office, a common-sense implementation, *PM Network*, 14(9), 94, September 2000.

Shenhar, A.J., The project management: the new framework, Proceedings of Portland International Conference on Management of Engineering and Technology, July 1999.

Sohmen, V. and Levin, G., Cross-cultural project communications embraces diversity, *ESI Horizons*, 3(6), November 2001.

Sriram, M., Developing a proposal for a PMO, *PM Network*, 14(8), 44, August 2000.

Stuckenbruck, L.C. and Marshall, D., *Team Building for Project Managers*, 3rd ed., Project Management Institute, Upper Darby, PA, 1990.

Whitten, N., Is your PMO respected? *PM Network*, 14(4), 21, April 2000.

INDEX

triple constraints, 5, 15
Vendor description, 25
Vice President of Projects, *see also*
        Competency requirements (by
        position); Duties (by position)
    description, 54-55
Virtual room, 139
Virtual teams, 168-171, 190, 191
Visibility room, 138 139

W

War room, 6, 136, 138-139, 169

Web sites
    PMI's Program Management Office
        Specific Interest Group, 125
    Standish Group, 35
    as visibility room, 139
Woodrow Wilson Bridge, 11
Workbook (project), 136, 140
Work breakdown structure (WBS)
    audit, 36
    maturity levels, 108, 112
    PMO implementation, 172, 173